SSR Paper 18

Security Sector Reform and Citizen Security: Experiences from Urban Latin America in Global Perspective

Robert Muggah and John de Boer

]u[
ubiquity press
London

DCAF Geneva Centre
for Security Sector
Governance
DCAF
Geneva

Published by
Ubiquity Press Ltd.
Unit 322-323
Whitechapel Technology Centre
75 Whitechapel Road
London E1 1DU
www.ubiquitypress.com

First published 2019

Cover image by Johnny Miller

Print and digital versions typeset by Siliconchips Services Ltd.

ISBN (Paperback): 978-1-911529-72-9
ISBN (PDF): 978-1-911529-73-6
ISBN (EPUB): 978-1-911529-74-3
ISBN (Mobi): 978-1-911529-75-0

Series: SSR Papers
ISSN (Print): 2571-9289
ISSN (Online): 2571-9297

DOI: https://doi.org/10.5334/bcc

The full text of this book has been peer-reviewed to ensure high academic standards. For full review policies, see http://www.ubiquitypress.com/

Suggested citation:
Muggah, R. and de Boer, J. 2019. *Security Sector Reform and Citizen Security: Experiences from Urban Latin America in Global Perspective*. London: Ubiquity Press. DOI: https://doi.org/10.5334/bcc. License: CC-BY 4.0

To read the free, open access version of this book online, visit https://doi.org/10.5334/bcc or scan this QR code with your mobile device:

Contents

SSR Papers

The DCAF SSR Papers provide original, innovative and provocative analysis on the challenges of security sector governance and reform. Combining theoretical insight with detailed empirically-driven explorations of state-of-the-art themes, SSR Papers bridge conceptual and pragmatic concerns. Authored, edited and peer reviewed by SSR experts, the series provides a unique platform for in-depth discussion of a governance-driven reform agenda, addressing the overlapping interests of researchers, policy-makers and practitioners in the fields of development, peace and security.

DCAF, the Geneva Centre for Security Sector Governance, is dedicated to making states and people safer. Good security sector governance, based on the rule of law and respect for human rights, is the very basis of development and security. DCAF assists partner states in developing laws, institutions, policies and practices to improve the governance of their security sector through inclusive and participatory reforms based on international norms and good practices.

About the Authors

Robert Muggah is a specialist in security, migration, and cities. In 2011 he co-founded the Igarapé Institute – a think and do tank working on data-driven safety and justice across Latin America and Africa. He also co-founded the SecDev Foundation and Group in 2008. For two decades he has advised national and municipal governments, the United Nations, World Bank and tech companies on issues ranging from arms control and crime prevention to urban planning and smart cities. He has worked extensively with DPKO, DPA, IOM, PBSO, UNDP, UNHCR and other agencies on related issues. Robert is a fellow or faculty at the University of Oxford, the University of San Diego, University of British Columbia, the Catholic University of Rio de Janeiro, the Graduate Institute Switzerland and Singularity University in San Francisco. He has published eight books and hundreds of policy and peer-reviewed articles including *Impact: Maps to Navigate Our Past and Future* (with Ian Goldin, forthcoming with Penguin/Random House in 2020), *Stability Operations, Security and Development* (New York: Routledge, 2013) and *Security and Post-Conflict Reconstruction: Dealing with Fighters in the Aftermath of War* (New York: Routledge, 2009). Robert received his Dphil from the University of Oxford and his MPhil from the University of Sussex.

John de Boer is the Managing Director of the SecDev Group, a strategic research advisory firm that works at the nexus of technology and social change. John has worked with the Canadian government, UN and a variety of think tanks and universities. He has advised numerous organizations and governments and has served as an expert for the UK Government's Expert Panel on Illicit Financial Flows, the International Federation of the Red Cross' World Disasters' Report 2016, the OECD's States of Fragility Report 2016. He was also an adviser to the UN Office on Drugs and Crime, UN Department of Political and Peacekeeping Affairs, the UN Office of Counter Terrorism, UN-Habitat, the UN World Humanitarian Summit, the OECD and the World Bank. He is author of dozens of peer-reviewed articles and books including *Reducing Urban Violence in the Global South: Towards Safe and Inclusive Cities* (Routledge, 2019) and *Safer Cities in the Global South: Engaging Social Theories of Urban Violence* (Routledge, 2018). John has a Ph.D. from the University of Tokyo.

Declaration

The views expressed in this publication do not in any way reflect the opinion or views of DCAF, the Geneva Centre for Security Sector Governance.

This book has been peer reviewed by multiple experts within the subject area. One of these peer reviewers is employed by DCAF but was not part of the editorial processes.

Acknowledgements

The authors would like to thank Christina Hoyos and Guy Lamb for conducting a thorough peer review of the paper.

Executive Summary

While widely considered a core pillar of the peace and security architecture, Security Sector Reform (SSR) is coming under fire. SSR theory and practice are criticized for being overly focused on traditional conflict and post-conflict settings and for being unable to adjust to unconventional settings marked by chronic crime and terrorism. SSR tends to be disproportionately focused on national institutions and less amenable to engaging at the subnational scale. Drawing on the experiences of so-called 'citizen security' measures in cities across Latin America and the Caribbean, this paper offers some opportunities for renewing and revitalizing SSR. The emphasis of citizen security interventions on multiple forms of insecurity, data-driven and evidence-informed prevention, the promotion of social cohesion and efficacy and designing crime prevention into the social and built environment are all insights that can positively reinforce comprehensive SSR measures in the 21st century.

Introduction

Security Sector Reform (SSR) is at a crossroads. SSR concepts and practices are embedded in international efforts to promote peace, security and development. They are widely considered an essential element of many multilateral and bilateral stabilization efforts and are a standard feature of the post-conflict toolkit.[1] SSR is routinely commended for the way it can integrate siloed fields of security, justice and development.[2] The centrality of SSR in peace support operations, political mandates and national efforts to build sustainable security institutions is frequently acknowledged in United Nations Security Council resolutions.[3] Moreover, the importance of ensuring civilian oversight over security institutions and delivering accountable public security is singled out in Goal 16 (peaceful and inclusive societies) of the UN's 2030 Agenda for Sustainable Development.[4] In theory, SSR´s position in the global peace and security architecture has never been more secure.

In spite of these noteworthy advances, the SSR concept and its track record are being seriously challenged by policy makers and scholars alike.[5] Failure to reform the security sectors of Afghanistan and Iraq have fueled doubts about the 'viability of the paradigm.'[6] Academics routinely criticize SSR for being too 'normative', 'utopian' and 'donor driven.'[7] SSR programs and projects are also regularly disparaged for being overly technocratic and emphasizing operational effectiveness at the expense of local context and the political dimensions of reform. Practitioners often bemoan the fact that donors too often favor a 'one-size-fits-all' approach to SSR.[8] What is more, the state-centric application of the SSR paradigm in mostly conflict-affected states has led to questions about the concept's utility for addressing both transnational and hyper-local challenges and for adapting to operational contexts that fall outside of the more conventional armed conflict and post-conflict environments.[9]

Several efforts are underway to help upgrade and transition SSR to overcome these challenges. Some analysts now refer to 'second generation SSR', wherein its normative characteristics are de-emphasized, there is greater openness to engaging with non-state security and customary justice

How to cite this book chapter:
Muggah, R. and de Boer, J. 2019. *Security Sector Reform and Citizen Security: Experiences from Urban Latin America in Global Perspective.* Pp. 1–2. London: Ubiquity Press. DOI: https://doi.org/10.5334/bcc.a.
License: CC-BY 4.0

institutions and there is more proactive engagement with urban and non-conflict contexts.[10] This paper aims to reinforce the evolution of next generation SSR by identifying lessons from settings outside conflict and post-conflict settings. It´s particular contribution is to examine the applicability of SSR and analogous constructs in urban settings marked by high levels of organized violent crime. The authors focus in on efforts to strengthen and reform security and justice institutions in Latin America and the Caribbean, a veritable laboratory of public security innovation over the past three decades.

Central to this paper is the connection between SSR and what is described as 'citizen security' across Latin America and the Caribbean. Ideas and practices associated with citizen security have informed national and subnational public security and criminal justice policies across the region for decades.[11] The construct emerged partly in opposition to state-centric models of security and crime prevention that emphasized repression and punitive norms over those privileging prevention and human rights. The authors contend that ideas and insights from citizen security could greatly enrich the next generation of SSR in cities and potentially outside of them. The former's emphasis on addressing multiple types of insecurity, emphasizing preventive measures based on a public health approach, introducing design changes to the social and built environment and engaging with notions of citizen co-existence and social cohesion are invaluable. A closer approximation could help renew and revitalize SSR so that it can better address challenges in unconventional settings, work with sub-national partners and contend with hyper-local realities that can rapidly unravel peace.[12]

There are many opportunities to integrate a citizen security approach into SSR and to learn from experimentation in cities, especially Latin America and the Caribbean. While there are obvious limits to replicating and adapting practices across distinct settings, this paper distils several insights that can potentially enhance the effectiveness of SSR from a citizen-centric perspective. This paper hones in on experiences in Latin America in particular, where the challenges are stark but the successful experiences are revealing. The first section sets out a short overview of the literature on SSR in the Americas. Section two explores the extent to which SSR policy and practice has evolved in cities. The third section explores the costs, causes and consequences of criminal violence in the region. In the process, it highlights several challenges confronting reform efforts in the Americas together with some promising entry-points. Section four explores the evolution of *mano dura* and citizen security. The fifth section draws attention to city-level citizen security experiences in Latin America and the Caribbean. The paper concludes with several recommendations for applying a citizen security lens to SSR.

SSR in the Americas

At its core, SSR is expected to reinforce measures that 'improve basic security and justice service delivery; establish an effective governance, oversight and accountability system; and develop local leadership and ownership of a reform process that enhances the technical capacity of the security system.'[13] SSR is most frequently deployed in post-conflict environments involving degraded state institutions and the proliferation of non-state security actors. Large-scale UN missions routinely included SSR programs, including in Afghanistan, Democratic Republic of Congo, East Timor, Haiti, Liberia and Nepal. SSR has also been introduced in political missions as a means of restoring state legitimacy from Burundi to Colombia.[14]

While not described as SSR, similar activities have been pursued across the Americas, where countries and cities experience widely diverging levels of security sector capacity. While nations such as Canada, Costa Rica and Chile have registered important gains in promoting civilian oversight over security institutions and promote accountable policing, justice and penal services, progress has been more incremental in Mexico, Central America and much of South America. Part of the challenge is that swathes of Latin America and the Caribbean feature exceedingly high levels of crime and victimization.[15] They also suffer from a chronic mistrust in public institutions, systemic social and economic inequalities and some of the most violent illicit markets in the world.

The history of security sector reform efforts in Latin America and the Caribbean can be traced to the latter half of the 20th century. They emerged largely in the wake of civil wars in El Salvador and Guatemala and the end of dictatorships in South America, most notably Argentina, Brazil and Chile. Some countries have been the site of repeated waves of security sector reform, including the Colombian government and various armed groups ranging from the Revolutionary Armed Forces of Colombia (FARC) to the AUC paramilitaries. National-level reforms have contributed to important gains in countries such as Argentina, Colombia and Peru. If measured by the extent

How to cite this book chapter:

Muggah, R. and de Boer, J. 2019. *Security Sector Reform and Citizen Security: Experiences from Urban Latin America in Global Perspective*. Pp. 3–5. London: Ubiquity Press. DOI: https://doi.org/10.5334/bcc.b. License: CC-BY 4.0

they have contributed to improving public security and reducing crime and corruption, such efforts were comparatively less successful in others, including in Brazil and the northern triangle countries of El Salvador, Guatemala and Honduras.[16]

Despite extensive efforts to reinforce civilian oversight over national security and justice institutions, parts of Latin America and the Caribbean are experiencing chronic security crises and impunity. In part, this was due to domestic political economies that privileged clientelism and patronage. In Guatemala, for example, many of the same elites that triggered war later resisted the implementation of structural changes to the national police and judiciary. The resulting dysfunction in the security sector there allowed space for the expansion of organized crime and associated violence.[17] Today, the number of absolute homicides is nearly double the toll of violent deaths experienced during the civil war in the 1980s.[18] Levels of gender-based violence have also increased dramatically.[19] While the particular historical experiences of countries across the region vary, they share a common challenge of rising violent crime and anxiety over insecurity. While most other countries in the world continue to benefit from the 'great crime decline'[20], Latin America remains caught in what some have called a 'high crime equilibrium'[21], fuelling an ugly cycle of insecurity and under-development.

During the late 1990s and early 2000s, Latin American and Caribbean governments began adopting more repressive and punitive approaches to containing spiralling crime and fighting drug trafficking.[22] The tendency toward militarized approaches to public security delivery—referred to as *mano dura* (or, iron fist)—expanded dramatically from Guatemala, El Salvador and Honduras to Brazil, Colombia, Mexico and Venezuela.[23] The resort to militarized solutions, the emphasis on restricting civil liberties and the resort to mass incarceration were hardly new strategies: they drew on the authoritarian legacies of governments across the region. Despite their popularity among socially conservative elements of Latin American and Caribbean societies, heavy-handed measures have had limited, even counter-productive, effects.[24] In spite of uneven improvements in overall democratic governance and social and economic well-being across the region, insecurity is deepening.

The fact is that conventional security sector reform efforts in Latin America and the Caribbean have struggled to take root. Top-down approaches to reforming security structures often encounter fierce resistance. On the one hand, newly democratic governments have either been unable or unwilling to undertake necessary and systemic reforms to military, law enforcement and criminal justice institutions. There are still elite interests, including those increasingly reliant on privatized security and overseas military assistance, to maintain an unequal and repressive status quo. On the other hand, Latin American and Caribbean societies still continue to endorse heavy-handed approaches to public security. With some exceptions, the armed forces are widely venerated (along with the Catholic Church), and fast-growing evangelical communities tend to support more conservative law and order positions. These factors are exacerbated by persistent levels of violence and victimization, a growing distrust of political institutions, the chronic un- and under-employment of young people, high levels of inequality and the presence of lucrative illicit markets.

Notwithstanding this challenging scenario, there are signs of alternative approaches emerging across Latin America and the Caribbean, particularly in the region's cities.[25] Even with uneven governance, gaping inequalities and massive unregulated urbanization, there are signs of cities developing successful strategies to promote safety and security at the municipal level.[26] Various efforts to reform security sectors at the urban scale—often described as citizen security—have been pursued since the 1990s, with some generating positive outcomes.[27] The emergence of citizen security efforts in cities is not a coincidence: more than 85 per cent of the region's population lives in an urban setting.[28] While national governments remain paramount in setting strategic priorities, owing to devolution programs implemented in the 1980s and 1990s, some municipal authorities exert a comparatively high degree of discretion and autonomy when it comes to public security delivery.[29]

For decades, cities in the Americas have been at the vanguard of experimenting with innovative approaches to reforming the security sector, even if not explicitly referred to as such. Under a variety of different guises—from citizen security to citizen co-existence—mayors, businesses and civic associations have explored alternative approaches to policing, delivering criminal justice and incarceration.[30] National, state and city authorities have rolled out security strategies that emphasize law and order on the one side and crime prevention and urban renewal (or what is called 'social urbanism' and 'urban acupuncture') on the other.[31] The focus is not only on restoring the legitimacy, credibility and capacity of public security institutions, but also on rebuilding an ethos of civic responsibility. This has entailed nurturing bottom-up strategies designed to restore social cohesion, social efficacy and the process of living together (*convivencia*). Cultivating a responsible, transparent and proactive reciprocal relationship between security and justice institutions and citizens is at the core of these efforts.

Not surprisingly, citizen-centric approaches to public security and justice delivery emerged out of the distinct historical experience of Latin America and the Caribbean.[32] They were a response to the legacy of military dictatorships and authoritarian rule of the 1960s–1980s. More recently, citizen security measures gained traction at the city scale as part of a popular rejection of violent involvement of military actors in domestic security provision.[33] Championed by mayors and civic leaders, citizen security encourages the creation of spaces for citizens to work together with police and state security forces to ensure more rights-respecting and community-facing security at the local level. Citizen security ideas and insights have also been amplified by inter-governmental entities, such as the Organization for American States (OAS), the Inter-American Development Bank (IADB) and the Latin American Development Bank (CAF), among others.[34] The extent to which citizen security discourse and practice has extended outside of Latin America and the Caribbean is harder to discern.[35]

Citizen security efforts have more recently been buoyed by several international standard setting efforts.[36] Important support came from the United Nations Development Program (UNDP) that has ramped-up support over the past decade, often in partnership with national and municipal governments.[37] Unrelated, the New Urban Agenda, adopted at the United Nations Conference on Housing and Sustainable Urban Development in 2016, also signalled the relationship between public security and cities. More recently, the sustainable development goals (SDGs), particularly commitments to promoting safer, more inclusive and resilient cities (SDG 11) and pledges to promote more peaceful and inclusive societies (SDG 16), are expected to add legitimacy and urgency to the spread of citizen-centric public security and criminal justice efforts from the national to the urban scale.

The SDGs, the New Urban Agenda and institutional support provided by the OAS, IADB, UNDP and others have helped legitimize citizen security measures adopted by municipal leaders across Latin America and the Caribbean (in particular). But their impact is potentially more far-reaching. Indeed, these agendas underline the ways in which security at the city scale is fundamentally connected to broader agendas of poverty reduction, inclusive governance, prosperity and sustainable development. They also potentially offer entry points for rethinking aspects of SSR with a citizen security lens. By including and moving beyond a narrow focus on the form and function of formal and informal security institutions, citizen security accounts for a wider interpretation of violence, a more comprehensive and balanced set of measures to improve safety and a broader network of partnerships spanning government, business and civil society.

SSR and Cities

Notwithstanding its successes, SSR is widely acknowledged as a concept in transition.[38] SSR has a long heritage, traced back to the reform of security forces in the wake of conflict and during periods of dramatic political transition throughout the 20th century. During the 1990s and 2000s, SSR was more tightly connected to post-conflict state-building exercises, including the Balkans, Iraq and Afghanistan. To leverage more development assistance and broaden SSR measures, the Organisation for Economic Co-operation and Development (OECD) issued an SSR framework in 2007 that emphasized how 'a democratically run, accountable and efficient security system [can help] reduce the risk of conflict, thus creating an enabling environment for development.'[39] The UN later formed the Inter-Agency Security Sector Reform Task Force to promote a 'comprehensive' UN approach and further anchor SSR as critical to the consolidation of peace and stability, the rule of law and good governance.[40] This framing helped SSR emerge as part of the 'standard toolbox of interventions in conflict affected states.'[41]

Although SSR concepts have been 'mainstreamed' into multilateral and bilateral assistance, many agencies and organizations have struggled to translate ambitious principles into reality.[42] The uneven outcomes of SSR programs and projects over the past decades have contributed to a growing chorus for 'radical change' to existing models.[43] Some of these calls have urged a greater emphasis on gender and local voices. Others have emphasized the importance of strengthening security system governance and pursuing more holistic reform processes. Likewise, there are increasing pressures to tailor SSR processes to subnational and even municipal realities.[44]

A recurring concern with SSR relates to the overly technocratic and mechanistic way it is often applied. There is often hesitation among policy makers and practitioners to fully acknowledge and engage with the deeply political nature of the endeavour.[45] To be truly effective, specialists claim that comprehensive SSR programming must go beyond improving the operational capability of the security forces and police and engage in more politically sensitive elements, including

How to cite this book chapter:
Muggah, R. and de Boer, J. 2019. *Security Sector Reform and Citizen Security: Experiences from Urban Latin America in Global Perspective.* Pp. 7–8. London: Ubiquity Press. DOI: https://doi.org/10.5334/bcc.c. License: CC-BY 4.0

parliamentary oversight, strengthening civil society engagement and ultimately reconfiguring power relations within the security sector and across government more broadly.[46] Successive World Bank and UN high-level reports on peacekeeping, peacebuilding and conflict prevention have likewise noted the importance of taking politics more fully into account.[47]

Another critique relates to the inability of SSR measures to appropriately adapt to local contexts and cultivate local ownership for reforms.[48] Indeed, most SSR initiatives have had limited engagement with non-state actors involved in providing security services to communities, cities and regions. SSR programs have long struggled with whether and how to interact with militias, community self-defence forces, private security companies, paramilitary groups and gangs.[49] Some analysts have encouraged SSR policy makers and practitioners to engage more closely with contexts and systems that exhibit layered, mixed or hybrid security orders. This requires negotiating in a more fulsome way with local security governance and sub-national factors that frequently shape security dynamics on the ground.[50]

The case to move beyond national institutions and processes and focus more on subnational institutions is bolstered by the phenomenal growth of cities. Cities are increasingly important political and economic actors, including in Africa, Asia and Latin America and the Caribbean. Already more than 55 per cent of the world's population lives in urban areas, and this is set to grow to 68 per cent by 2050. The pace of unregulated urbanization is particularly pronounced in fragile and conflict-affected countries.[51] Agencies ranging from the United Nations to the OECD[52] have started drawing attention to the need to promote more integrated and inclusive measures to promote urban safety and the prevention of crime and terrorism in cities.[53] SDG 11, which focuses on cities, has reinforced the need for development and security actors to engage cities as a core element of the sustainable development agenda.[54]

Owing to the fact that SSR efforts have traditionally focused on national institutions, their relationship with cities have not received much attention. Indeed, multilateral and bilateral agencies are often legally required to work with centralized entities. Those studies that have engaged with the urban dimensions of SSR have struggled to identify 'a unique urban security system.'[55] A prevailing assumption is that urban realities are typically a microcosm of national dynamics (though it is also the case that some rural areas are also intensely neglected and suffer from heightened insecurity). Yet, this lack of engagement with SSR in cities constitutes a gap in the SSR literature. This is certainly the case in Latin America and the Caribbean, one of the world's most urbanized regions where insecurity is an uppermost concern among residents. This does not mean that security sector innovations, and citizen security measures more specifically, are not actively pursued. There are hundreds of examples of efforts to reinforce the legitimacy, credibility and capacity of municipal and metropolitan public security institutions, coupled with parallel efforts to strengthen civic participation and social cohesion at the neighborhood level.[56]

Consequences, Causes and Costs of Insecurity in Latin America and the Caribbean

Latin America and the Caribbean is the world's most violent region when measured by the prevalence and absolute toll of lethal and non-lethal violence.[57] In 2017, the region accounted for 38 per cent of all violent deaths and just 14 per cent of the global population.[58] The regional homicide rate of 22 per 100,000 is three times the global average. El Salvador, Jamaica, Venezuela and Honduras ranked top four in homicide rates per 100,000, while Brazil, Colombia, Mexico and Venezuela registered the highest absolute numbers of homicides at over 63,000, 11,000, 25,000 and 16,000, respectively, in 2017.[59] Taken together, since 2000, more than 2.5 million Latin Americans have been killed violently with the majority of these deaths firearm-inflicted and the result of gang-related violence.[60] Latin America also registers some of the highest levels of reported physical assault and violent robbery in the world. Crime and victimization are consistently ranked by residents as their primary concern, and Latin Americans are the least likely of any other population group to report feeling safe.[61]

While the overall levels of organized and interpersonal violence are high, there is nevertheless significant heterogeneity across Latin America and the Caribbean. In parts of Central America and the Caribbean sub-region, for example, homicide rates are three to four times higher than the global average, though they are subject to fluctuation as recent declines in El Salvador, Guatemala and Honduras show.[62] Meanwhile, in countries such as Argentina, Chile, Ecuador, Costa Rica and Peru, levels of lethal violence are lower than the global average. In Mexico and the Northern Triangle countries of El Salvador, Guatemala and Honduras, violence and population displacement have soared (though declined in recent years).[63] Drug trafficking organizations, such as the Sinaloa Cartel and the Zetas, as well as gangs, such as MS-13 and Barrio 18, are singled out

How to cite this book chapter:
Muggah, R. and de Boer, J. 2019. *Security Sector Reform and Citizen Security: Experiences from Urban Latin America in Global Perspective*. Pp. 9–14. London: Ubiquity Press. DOI: https://doi.org/10.5334/bcc.d. License: CC-BY 4.0

for as much as one third of the lethal violence (measured as 'collective homicide') in the Americas, compared to less than one per cent in Asia or Europe.[64] The high rates of such violence are often put down to competition over political and economic rents, ineffective criminal justice systems, weak enforcement practices and high levels of impunity.[65]

The economic costs of organized crime and interpersonal violence run into the hundreds of billions of dollars across the region. Part of the reason for this is due to the comparatively high public and private expenditures on crime control, but it is also due to the loss of productive life resulting from the premature death and injury of young males. The total costs of criminal violence—measured as a function of public expenditures and lost productivity for 17 countries in Latin America—are estimated by the Inter-American Development Bank to amount to between US\$114.5 and US\$170.4 billion a year.[66] This amounts to a US\$300 per capita tax on all citizens if measured using nominal GDP values. The costs vary from place to place: in Trinidad and Tobago and the Bahamas, the crime tax reaches US\$1,189 and US\$1,176 per capita, respectively. By comparison, in countries like Argentina, Chile, Brazil and El Salvador, the costs are double the regional (per capita) average.[67] All told, the economic burden of crime in the region is more than double the average costs in developed OECD countries.[68]

Latin America's organized violence problem is the subject of considerable debate. Latin America is justifiably praised for establishing a regional 'zone of peace'.[69] The region has not experienced an inter-state war since 1998. It is true that the region suffered at least 14 civil wars since the end of the Second World War. Nevertheless, the last remaining internal conflict officially came to an end with the 2016 peace deal between the Colombian state and the FARC. Negotiations with the remaining guerrilla group of Colombia, the ELN, have stalled. Notwithstanding dangerous political and economic volatility in Venezuela, including the threat of complete collapse[70], and occasional constitutional crises, Latin America has effectively rid the region of warfare. These successes were due in large part to the spread of democratic governance, real economic gains and periodic interventions from regional organizations and so-called 'guarantor states'.[71]

While organized crime and criminal violence are widely distributed across Latin America and the Caribbean, they tend to concentrate in urban settings, especially peripheral informal areas where state presence is weak. In 2017, more than 41 of the 50 most murderous cities in the world were located in Latin America.[72] Roughly 170 of Latin America's cities with populations of 250,000 or more registered homicide rates above 25 per 100,000 people.[73] Some of the region´s fastest growing cities, such as Acapulco in Mexico, Caracas in Venezuela, Maceió in Brazil and San Pedro Sula in Honduras, are particularly affected by chronic crime and victimization. Even in cities

Table 1. *Changes in homicide rates (murders per 100,000 inhabitants) by region: 2000–2017.*

	2000	2003	2008	2013	2017	D 17 years	D 15 years	D 10 years	D 5 years
Africa	11	10	9	8.4	8.0	-25%	-22%	-11%	-6%
Asia	3	3	2	2.3	1.9	-40%	-35%	-22%	-15%
Europe	8	7	4	2.8	2.4	-68%	-67%	-32%	-14%
Oceania	3	3	3	2.8	2.6	-10%	-23%	-9%	-9%
North America	16	16	15	15.7	15.7	0%	-3%	2%	0%
Latin American	22	23	21	22.2	21.9	-1%	-3%	3%	-2%
Global estimate	6	6	5	5.1	4.8	-25%	-23%	-9%	-6%

Source: Aguirre and Muggah (2018) – D stands for change over time.

that are viewed to be comparatively 'safe', such as Buenos Aires, Lima or Montevideo, feelings of insecurity are soaring due to high levels of victimization.

Although sharing common characteristics, different cities experience distinct spatial, demographic and temporal patterns of crime and victimization. In some cities—Acapulco, Belem or San Salvador—there are comparatively high levels of lethal violence, much of it perpetrated by organized groups. Meanwhile, in other cities, such as Quito or Sao Paulo, rates of lethal violence are relatively low despite the presence of organized groups.[74] The expression of criminal violence is invariably shaped by the political economy of crime and the relative capacity of the state. Other factors that may shape the severity of crime include the types of illicit markets involved (conflict over their control as well as the means of financing conflict), the organizational characteristics of the groups implicated in crime, the security strategies pursued by state agencies and the resulting equilibrium or disequilibrium in informal markets.

Notwithstanding tremendous heterogeneity, there are also shared characteristics of organized criminal violence in Latin America. While trends in violence and victimization fluctuate, they nevertheless tend to concentrate in specific locations.[75] Crime and victimization are frequently concentrated in particular cities and within certain neighborhoods and blocks or 'hot spots'.[76] In most locations, the largest share of violence occurs on just a few street corners where there tends to be a high degree of social disorganization, institutional anomie, concentrated disadvantage and population flux. In Honduras, for example, more than two thirds of all homicides occur in just three cities.[77] Meanwhile, in Bogotá, researchers found that around just one per cent of the city's streets accounted for 98 per cent of its lethal victimization in 2012–2013.[78] This type of crime concentration is in fact common in many urban settings around the world.[79]

There are also several common demographic features to criminal violence in Latin America. For one, young, poorer and minority males comprise the overwhelming majority of victims of homicide in countries such as Brazil, Colombia, El Salvador, Honduras, Mexico and Venezuela. Likewise, in countries such as Bolivia, Guatemala and Peru, indigenous populations are also unevenly targeted by state- and private sector-motivated violence in rural areas.[80] Living in areas of concentrated disadvantage, with comparatively low access to health care, education, labor markets and basic infrastructure, compounds the risk of victimization.[81] Indigenous women and girls are particularly vulnerable to exploitation and abuse, including sexual violence, especially where homicide rates are already high.[82] Indeed, femicide is a particularly worrying concern in countries such as Guatemala.[83]

There are many theories seeking to explain why criminal violence tends to cluster in certain places and among certain people. Some scholars argue that specific neighborhoods within cities offer opportunities for criminal activity as a result of political neglect and the absence of state presence, together with localized economic decay.[84] Related, insights from social disorganization theory connect higher crime rates with areas exhibiting a higher density of offenders, a higher percentage of rental housing and large social housing projects.[85] Indeed, the probability of becoming involved in crime increases if one is raised in a high-crime affected zone.[86] These findings are reinforced by Patrick Sharkey's recent work that documented how violent crime was concentrated at far higher levels in the most 'disadvantaged and disconnected' areas of cities.[87] More broadly, research is increasingly demonstrating that urban violence is multi-factoral.[88] The cumulative effects of overlapping political, social, economic and environmental risks drive many forms of criminal violence and victimization in cities.[89]

Causes of organized violence in the Americas

Why is criminal violence so persistent in Latin American cities? It is likely several factors that influence the scale and dynamics of lethal and non-lethal violence in Latin America and the

Caribbean.[90] Scholars have isolated a host of structural risks that are tightly correlated with intentional homicide.[91] Among these are inequality, unemployment among young males, low quality education, high impunity rates and social norms condoning violence against women and girls.[92] Other triggers include rapid unregulated urbanization, the systemic penetration of organized crime and gangs who are disputing control over illicit economies, the drugs trade (and inelasticity of cocaine consumption) and the ready access to alcohol and firearms availability.[93]

Part of the reasons for the sustained levels of criminal violence relate to stubbornly high rates of economic and social inequality in Latin America and the Caribbean.[94] This is consistent with research in other regions as well, where the association between crime and inequality often holds. Globally, crime rates tend to be higher in unequal cities.[95] There are several reasons why greater inequality corresponds with a higher likelihood of criminal violence. For one, large disparities in wealth create greater competition in and between populations experiencing high unemployment and limited upward mobility. What is more, income inequality tends to reinforce 'public goods traps' that can reinforce weak service delivery (including law and order) in low-income areas.

While the region as a whole has seen some incremental improvements in income equality, the World Bank and the Socio-Economic Database for Latin America and the Caribbean (SEDLAC) detected reversals in inequality in parts of Central America's northern triangle and the Andean region.[96] The fact is that Latin America registers the most unequal distribution of income on the planet: including 8 of the 20 most unequal countries in the world.[97] On average, the region has a Gini inequality of 41 in relation to wage inequality as compared to the OECD average of 31.8.[98] Yet, inequality only tells part of the story. When measures of poverty are included in models to examine homicide, the inequality-homicide effect diminishes substantially.[99]

Another factor influencing high homicide and violent crime rates is persistent youth unemployment. The average rate of youth unemployment in the region was 19.5 per cent in 2017. This was equivalent to 10 million youth, or one in every five youths, without access to work.[100] More unemployed males often means more violence. In parts of Brazil, for example, a one per cent increase in the unemployment rate for men results in a two per cent spike in murder.[101] This could also be linked to the explosion of 'aspirational crime', whereby young people unable to access material goods see crime as the only way to experience the consumer lifestyle. Those either perpetrating or suffering from homicide are typically young people who are unemployed, under-educated and lacking options.[102]

The sheer scale and dimensions of violence against women suggest that it is widely tolerated in many Latin American and Caribbean societies. Social scientists often describe such attitudes as 'normalized' within societies across the region. Indeed, gender-based violence is prolific: 14 of the 24 countries with the highest rates of femicide are in Latin America.[103] Domestic violence rates reach 50 per cent of all women in some countries.[104] The characteristics of violence against women differ in several respects from that committed against men. Women are more commonly physically assaulted by known acquaintances, family members and intimate partners. They are also more frequently sexually assaulted and exploited at childhood, during adolescence and as adults. Factors that aggravate sexual violence are connected to unequal gender social orders and power relations between men and women. Specifically, the legitimization of violence against women, blaming of women for rape and other forms of sexual violence, viewing women as sexual objects and the cult of women's virginity are all singled out.[105]

Weak security and justice institutions are also associated with high rates of crime and violence.[106] When police, prosecutors, defenders, judges and penal authorities exhibit low institutional legitimacy and uneven capacity, the costs of crime decline. This is because low institutional capacity to deliver law and order corresponds with clientelism, patronage and impunity. In Latin America, just 20 of every 100 homicides results in conviction. This compares to a global clearance rate of

43 out of 100.[107] In Brazil, the ratio is just 5 of every 100 homicides. There are several explanations for institutional weakness in the law enforcement and criminal justice sectors. The legacy of civil war and military rule in countries like Argentina, Brazil, Colombia, El Salvador and Haiti are at least partly to blame. Military and police institutions continue operating with an institutional culture that celebrates martial traditions. Likewise, armed forces, intelligence services and police departments still enable clandestine structures that may undertake extra-judicial operations.[108]

A key factor shaping systemic impunity is organized crime, especially drug production, transit and trafficking. The three major cocaine-producing countries are all located in South America: notably, Bolivia, Colombia and Peru. Virtually every single Latin American and Caribbean country is affected to varying degrees by drug cartels and splinter factions that manage at least US$330 billion in annual revenues.[109] In many countries, such groups have not just infiltrated the military, law enforcement and criminal justice system, but also they have penetrated the executive, legislative and judicial arms of government. A weakened state is an ideal environment for organized crime. Coopting public institutions is often much more efficient than fighting them directly. Moreover, many drug trafficking organizations shift considerable resources from the illicit to the licit economy through pyramid schemes, real estate ventures, building construction and financial campaigns. Put simply, the drug economy spills over into the real economy, employing literally millions of people and driving massive private security industries across the region.

Promoting institutional reform in a way that enhances the performance, transparency and accountability of military and police has been an area of priority for SSR practitioners. Yet, security and justice sector institutions in the region seem to have been caught up in a vicious circle of 'high crime and weak state capabilities'.[110] As the opportunities for illicit rents grow, state institutions struggle to keep pace. In some cases, state institutions and political leaders facilitate and profit from crime through corrupt practices. Corruption has corroded the integrity of public office and institutions. Over the past decade, corruption scandals have brought down over 6 former presidents and 300 elected federal and state officials in Brazil, 6 elected presidents in Guatemala, President Pedro Pablo Kuczynski of Peru and former presidents in Argentina, El Salvador, Guatemala and Honduras.[111]

Levels of trust in state institutions are shockingly low. Only 2 in 10 people across the region have high levels of faith in their government. For Brazil, Chile, Costa Rica, Colombia, Paraguay and Peru, the number is closer to 1 in 10. Public opinion surveys consistently rank the capacity and integrity of judicial institutions, police and public servants (municipal and national) exceptionally low. Some 44 per cent of Latin Americans believe that the police are involved in crime. In Buenos Aires, less than 20 per cent of the population trust the police.[112] In Lima and La Paz, that figure is less than 10 per cent and in Caracas 15 per cent.[113] Social cohesion, trust and a shared commitment to the community are critical to violence reduction and social development in crime-ridden neighbourhoods.

There are many other reasons that Latin American and Caribbean countries are contending with excessive violence. For example, the abundance of unlicensed firearms, including those trafficked from the US or leaked domestically, are also associated with the region's disproportionately high burden of gun violence.[114] Not surprisingly, Latin American countries and cities are among the world's most prone to gun-related violence. Approximately 75 per cent of all homicides in Latin America are caused by firearms, compared to the global average of roughly 42 per cent. In Brazil and Honduras, the percentage of gun-related murders soars close to 90 per cent. Handguns and assault rifles are not the cause of homicide or violent crime, but their abundance and easy accessibility certainly increase the risk of a fatal outcome during disputes between intimate partners, holdups or encounters between rival gangs. And while weaponry is trafficked illegally from outside the region, the most common source is much closer to home: local military and police arsenals. Weapons are routinely pilfered from the current stocks of the armed forces and police.[115]

What all this means is that in Latin American cities, insecurity has emerged as the principle concern and crime avoidance has become an important characteristic of behaviour for many individuals and communities. People have modified how and when they move in the city, children have been prevented from attending school, those that can afford private security have built up fortresses and those who cannot have developed coping strategies that include vigilantism, joining gangs or self-help community groups. Millions have also chosen, or were forced, to migrate elsewhere. Without significant investments in building public trust in state security institutions and in improving their effectiveness, these trends will likely continue.

From *Mano Dura* to Citizen Security

The spread of *mano dura* measures in Latin America and the Caribbean

Mano dura policies and practices include the application of repression to achieve public order. It often entails the excessive use of military and police force to address common crime in cities and their peripheries. For much of the past century, Latin American and Caribbean governments have adopted heavy-handed approaches to crime control and public security. Many countries across the region emerged from dictatorships and civil wars during the 1970s and 1980s with their military and paramilitary institutions left intact. Some continued to rely on their armed forces and paramilitary forces to maintain law and order. A number of countries also introduced legislative changes allowing for the criminalization of misdemeanors, and courts regularly accepted extrajudicial confessions, the detention of suspects without charge, and crack-downs during declared 'emergencies'. Inmates are often detained for years without access to counsel. The principle objective of most regimes was self-preservation above the protection of people and their civil rights and freedoms.

The persistence of *mano dura* style policies and practices to the present day is a result of several factors. For one, historically high crime rates have ensured that 'tough on crime' responses stay at the top of the political agenda. Hard-line populist and ultra-conservative politicians, backed by media, faith-based groups and business interests, have frequently sought to maintain the status quo. Not surprisingly, elected officials routinely increase military and police crack-downs and mass incarceration in response to citizen anxieties over crime and personal insecurity. Recent surveys show that public concerns with rising crime and victimization are also positively correlated with increasing support for authoritarian government,[116] due process restrictions, expanded police discretion and informal justice.[117]

Despite increasing evidence that *mano dura* approaches to security do not work, the majority of Latin Americans (61 per cent) favour punitive approaches to public security.[118] As Table 2

How to cite this book chapter:
Muggah, R. and de Boer, J. 2019. *Security Sector Reform and Citizen Security: Experiences from Urban Latin America in Global Perspective.* Pp. 15–22. London: Ubiquity Press. DOI: https://doi.org/10.5334/bcc.e.
License: CC-BY 4.0

demonstrates, this also coincides with the high levels of confidence that the public has in its armed forces as compared to the police and other institutions of government. This viewpoint is consistent across the entire region regardless of whether the country suffers from high or low crime rates.[119] This sentiment has been accompanied by a tendency toward the militarization of police functions and repressive tactics across the region to restore public order. Honduras, El Salvador, Nicaragua, Colombia and even Brazil have witnessed this first-hand. In El Salvador, the number of military personnel deployed in cities has increased from 876 to 13,827 over the past two decades.[120]

A range of criminological and sociological theories tentatively back *mano dura*, or at least strongly punitive, policies. For example, 'zero tolerance' approaches to crime prevention in North America[122] are positively viewed across the region and widely endorsed by many right-leaning politicians and police chiefs in Latin America and the Caribbean. Despite uneven evidence of positive effects[123], public authorities routinely cite such approaches, and particularly the New York experience of the 1990s, as a justification for ratcheting up repression. Yet, unlike police-led efforts in North America, Latin American efforts to introduce zero tolerance exert few formal checks and

Table 2. *Confidence in institutions across Latin America (2015–2018).*

	2015	2016	2018
Church	69	66	63
Armed forces	44	50	44
Police	36	38	35
Electoral institutions	44	32	28
Government	33	28	23
Judicial system	30	26	22
Congress	27	26	21
Political parties	20	17	13

Source: Corporación Latinobarómetro (2018)[121]

Table 3. *Characteristics of mano dura approaches.*

	Law enforcement	Courts	Penal
Cracking down on low level offenders and offences	Aggressive operations, arrests for minor offences, continual harassment	Changing laws to criminalize misdemeanors and some behaviors, mandatory sentencing laws	Preventive detention, arbitrary imprisonment of youths
Reduction and suspension of procedural rights	Unauthorized searches, forced confessions, increase of discretionary faculties	Extra-judicial confessions, pre-trial detention, lowered evidentiary standards	Reducing criminal age of responsibility and segregating gang leaders
Deployment of military and forceful policing	Deployment of military, use of paramilitary, massive police crackdowns, tolerance of vigilantism	Emergency laws suspending civil liberties and expanding military and police powers	Use of military prisons, use of severe punishments

Source: Muggah and Garzon (2018)

balances. What is more, punitive measures are often rolled out in situations where criminal justice institutions are weak and where police officers are poorly trained.[124]

Practically speaking, *mano dura* policies can be summarized as three sets of measures (see Table 3). It is their combination, and not necessarily just the application of one set of activities on their own, that demarcates *mano dura* from strict zero tolerance style approaches to crime prevention and criminal justice.

At the outset, there is the expansion of police discretion to search and arrest suspects on the basis of limited evidence and the imposition of criminal sentences for minor offences. One result is that police are granted a license to dramatically expand activities in poor and marginal neighborhoods. They can search, seize and arrest people for civil misdemeanors ranging from loitering, public nuisance, and vagrancy to, more ambiguously, 'no licit purposes' or 'lacking an identity document'. Because the target of many *mano dura* approaches are 'gangs—from well-organized *maras* to street-corner cliques—the result is often a speedy and far-reaching imprisonment of young people.

Mano dura style legislation is common throughout Central America, especially El Salvador, Guatemala and Honduras. It is not only associated with the 'war on drugs' discourse, but also with the logic of 'counter-terrorism' and 'war on terror' since 9/11. In October 2006, for example, El Salvador initiated the *Special Law Against Acts of Terrorism*. A decade later, after abandoning a truce with gangs, public authorities passed new anti-gang measures classifying gangs as terrorist organizations. And in Honduras, in 2015, the government tightened its legislation to confront gang activity by imposing stricter prison sentencing and new legal tools for prosecuting gang members. Shortly thereafter, in 2017, Guatemalan legislators proposed a similar bill to the one introduced in El Salvador and Honduras. It criminalized the country's gangs by increasing penalties and prison sentences for suspected affiliates.

The extreme use of force by police in many Latin American and Caribbean countries is systemic and corrosive. The Latinbarómeter, for example, has documented how Argentina, El Salvador, Bolivia and Colombia report the highest levels of police abuse.[125] The police use of force can escalate overall levels of violence: there is a positive relationship between a country's murder rate and the overall share of killings committed by the police.[126] Although some commentators argue that these high ratios might be the result of Latin American and Caribbean police officers facing frequent dangerous encounters, recent evidence suggests that the ratio of people killed by police to police officers killed by suspects in such places is higher than 10:1, implying the serious misuse of force.[127]

Next, there is a significant erosion of the procedural rights that are guaranteed to suspects, including young people (under 18). *Mano dura* style interventions often include a litany of abuses, including pre-trial detention, extrajudicial confessions, the watering down of protections for minors, the lowering of the age of criminal responsibility, an increased prevalence of unauthorized searches and lowered evidentiary standards. There are also frequently efforts to segregate and contain prisoners once they are in jails, often with highly counterproductive results.

Because of the lack of restraints on police abuse or procedural guarantees for detainees, these *mano dura* measures extend beyond zero tolerance strategies.

Mano dura approaches often infringe on the fundamental rights of suspects, especially young, low-income minorities. Hyper-aggressive policing is endemic, including stop and searches, as are more concerted measures targeting at-risk youth. In Nicaragua, for example, the Inter-American Human Rights Commission has reported significant arbitrary detentions and restrictions limiting access of detainees to legal representation.[128] Protests there have been criminalized, and analysts are concerned about the balance of power within the armed forces between those loyal to President Ortega and the military.[129] Reports of parapolice groups, allegedly composed of gang members, plain-clothed police and members of the Sandinista Youth have also surfaced. The parapolice are accused of participating in kidnapping, extortion and looting private businesses.[130]

Another common feature of *mano dura* is the extension of prison sentences for both violent and non-violent offences. The logic is that stiff sentencing and robust detention will deter future perpetration of crime. There is, however, limited evidence that such measures are effective as a deterrent. Neither does it appear that longer and more severe prison terms contribute to reducing recidivism and re-offending. To the contrary, stronger penalties may reverse, and even strengthen, the power of organized crime, including prison gangs, with youth membership.[131] From Colombia, Brazil and Mexico to Guatemala, El Salvador and Honduras, prisons have provided ideal staging grounds not just for the recruitment of young gang members, but also for enhancing their cohesiveness and sharing skills to commit further crimes.

Mass incarceration policies and prison overcrowding is common across the region. Latin America has one of the world's highest average rate of incarceration at 261 per 100,000 residents. In the case of El Salvador, that number is 492 per 100,000, ranking it the 7th highest in the world. The total prison population of Central American countries has risen by over 80 per cent since 2000. In South America, Brazil has the largest prison population at over 712,000 people (the 3rd largest total prison population in the world).[132] Conditions in many of these prisons are extreme, with official occupancy rates well over capacity. In Bolivia, the occupancy level is above 250 per cent, in Peru over 220 per cent and in Brazil 165 per cent.[133] In Guatemala and El Salvador, the average overcrowding rate is 333 per cent. Some report figures of overcapacity as high as 902 per cent in some of El Salvador's prisons.[134] Prisons in El Salvador have averaged 39 deaths a year since 2015, with a significant number dying due to outbreaks of tuberculosis. In many cases, the horrendous conditions have caused prison riots. In fact, 32 of El Salvador's prisons are now under extraordinary security measures to restore order.

The dramatic surge in prison populations is a function of stricter penalties and longer sentences, rather than simply increased apprehensions. Repressive policies that disproportionately criminalize the poor and first-time drug offenders are part of the problem.[135] Mass incarceration has negative social and economic consequences outside prisons, including increasing poverty[136] and corroding neighborhood systems of social control and social support by, for instance, breaking up families, negatively affecting the conditions of communities, increasing reliance on government welfare and heightening barriers to legitimate work opportunities.[137] It is important also to note that Latin America has the second highest proportion of women incarcerated in the world.[138] Most of them are charged on drug-related offences, especially serving as mules. What is more, female imprisonment has increased over 200 per cent during the past two decades.[139] This issue continues to be neglected, despite the far-reaching psychological, physical, familial and economic burdens such imprisonments generate.

Finally, there is the deployment of highly militarized police and the armed forces to secure domestic security. The involvement of heavily armed troops in crime prevention reverses decades of efforts to promote security sector reform through enhanced civilian oversight and investment in law enforcement and criminal justice systems. While most constitutions allow the deployment of military during national crises as a temporary measure for exceptional circumstances, *mano dura* condones the more permanent use of military assets to control organized crime, including gangs, ostensibly to promote peace and order.[140] Despite years of institutional reforms, the entrenchment of democratic governance over the security sector has yet to be achieved. Not only do governments often lack the political will to implement reforms, but also police corporations are frequently skeptical and resist change.[141] As a result, regressive organizational cultures persist, many of them committed to heavy-handed repressive approaches to policing.

From Brazil and Colombia to El Salvador and Mexico, there are countless examples of how governments deploy military and paramilitary assets to fight crime. The effects of using the armed forces to stabilize crime-affected areas and deterring specific perpetrators of crime are mixed. On the one hand, there are occasions where the use of soldiers to pacify, occupy, and contain can have a temporary anesthetic effect. However, these tactics, alongside counter-narcotics and counter-insurgency measures more generally, can also contribute to the widespread and routine violation of human rights, including state killings, disappearances, torture and overall increases in violent mortality in the medium- to long-term. In Brazil, over 6,100 people were killed by the police in 2018[142], up from approximately 4,000 in 2016.[143] In El Salvador, the percentage of murders attributed to the police increased from less than 1 per cent in 2010 (121 of 4,004 homicides) to almost 5 per cent in 2015 (328 of 6,656) and more than 10 per cent by 2017 (412 of 3,954).[144]

There is growing recognition among many public security experts and a collection of public authorities across Latin America that more balanced strategies are required. Some governments, notably Colombia, Mexico and Uruguay, have also experimented with limited regulation of certain drugs, together with intelligence-led policing (ILP)[145] and preventive measures with positive results.[146] At the core of many efforts to promote responsible and transparent security and justice institutions in the region are citizens, and these efforts will be described in the section that follows.

Lessons from citizen security for SSR

Citizen security includes a set of ideas and activities designed to prevent and reduce violence, promote public security and access to justice, reinforce social cohesion and guarantee the mutual rights and obligations of states and citizens. In principle, citizen security entails the delivery of effective public safety measures in the context of broader democratic norms. It is distinct from and broader than punitive law and order approaches to policing and crime control. It is also broader than SSR because it includes interventions, such as urban infrastructure renewal, civic education and hotspot and community policing. While a popular concept in policy circles, citizen security has been comparatively under-theorized by scholars. Even so, the term has caught on in the Americas, with most countries now laying claim to a national or subnational citizen security policy, and virtually all international donors describe at least some of their investments in the same way.

There is growing investment in citizen security strategies precisely because they appear to have reigned in the more violent instincts of states. Citizen security policies and programs are supported by donor governments, international agencies and civil society groups precisely because of their focus on guaranteeing human rights and civil liberties.[147] This is not to suggest that citizen security appeals to all quarters of society: to the contrary, there are conservative elements that remain hostile, seeing it as 'soft on crime' or a wider project of the Left. Regardless, fundamental to the concept are two basic ideas that have gained traction across Latin America: the responsible state and active citizenship.

The first pillar of citizen security is the responsible state. Consistent with the literature on security sector reform and human security, for example, citizen security considers states have the ultimate responsibility to protect their citizens and to ensure basic guarantees of their safety and well-being. And yet, in many Latin American cities and outlying slums, the state has either been unable or unwilling to abide by this basic obligation. Security entities are alternately predatory or negligent. Not surprisingly, public confidence in state institutions, especially police, courts and prisons, has reached historic lows.

The second of these concepts is active citizenship. It is not just police, but also citizens that play a key role in ensuring their own security. On the one hand, citizens hold state officials to account for their failures to provide security. On the other hand, the success of many public safety policies is predicated on positive engagement between police and the wider population. Finding ways of building engagement between the police and the population, including measures to promote more accountable and community-oriented approaches, is essential in delivering information and building and implementing effective policing policy. Ultimately citizens, in collaboration with law enforcement, must take ownership of their own security. This does not imply support for vigilantism or lynching as is alarmingly common in some parts of Latin America and the Caribbean.[148]

Neither does it imply the creation of militia or paramilitary forces or investing in more prisons that are often referred to as 'crime colleges'.

At heart, citizen security is mediated by the state but guided and implemented with active public involvement. Citizen security is consistent with, though not substituted by, a wide variety of successful policing practices across the globe, including problem-oriented policing, proximity and community-oriented policing and ILP.[149] Such approaches are often introduced in the context of police reform and modernization in Latin America.[150] In addition to specific policing strategies and tactics, citizen security policies also encompass an array of activities seeking to improve general safety, prevent violence and reduce crime. These can include, but are not limited to, the redesign and upgrade of urban spaces (environmental design), job creation, vocational training, employment placement programs, educational measures and school-based interventions, early childhood and parent support activities and formal and informal mediation to reduce inter-group tensions in highly volatile situations.

Latin American and Caribbean countries and international partners have broadened their strategy for dealing with gangs and consciously emphasize regional and citizen security-oriented solutions. For example, there have been multiple regional, national and city-based efforts to introduce comprehensive approaches over the past decade, with a focus on preventive programs and reinsertion projects to address ex-gang members and at-risk youth. International agencies have also expanded cooperation with national counterparts to promote prevention and rehabilitation programs, community policing support and ad hoc arrangements focused on reinsertion and rehabilitation efforts for at-risk and actual gang members at the municipal level.[151] The United States Agency for International Development (USAID), for example, has supported a rash of municipal programs with Central American governments to address chronic youth unemployment, the promotion of educational opportunities and strategies to deal with inter-familial and intimate partner violence. These efforts have been complemented with outreach centers, strengthening juvenile justice systems and citizen action through local diagnostics.[152]

Citizen security also poses a challenge to private security, a booming business across Latin America.[153] Globally, private security is worth between US$140 and US$180 billion annually, though it is difficult to obtain precise figures.[154] The number of private security personnel across Latin America outstrips police officers by a ratio of at least 2:1, and this rises much higher in some countries, such as Brazil, Colombia, El Salvador, Honduras and Mexico.[155] While they are increasingly connected to local political economies across the region, in both the formal and informal sectors, there are open questions about the degree of protection generated by armed guards. Few countries in the region have regulatory mechanisms in place to control, monitor and sanction private security personnel. There is little coordination between private security firms and the national police, particularly in terms of firearm authorization, training and the reporting of crimes. There are also concerns with the corrosive effects of the spread of private security on public spending for security and safety.[156] Latin American elites show limited appetite to subsidize public security services, especially given their low trust in police and justice institutions.

Table 4. *Strategic focus of citizen security (1998–2016, n: 1,300).*

	Interventions
Common Crime	839
Gender Crime	192
Juvenile Crime	363
Organized Crime	180
State crime	5

Source: Igarapé Institute, *Citizen Security Dashboard*.

Table 5. *Levels of focus of citizen security in Latin America (1998–2016, n: 1,300).*

	Interventions
City	347
National	537
Regional	229
State	152

Source: Igarapé Institute, *Citizen Security Dashboard*.

Table 6. *Geographic distribution of citizen security in Latin America (1998–2016, n: 1,300).*

	Interventions
Regional	271
Sub-regional	229
Brazil	202
Guatemala	100
Nicaragua	81
Honduras	69
El Salvador	65
Trinidad and Tobago	31
Mexico	29
Chile	29
Jamaica	24
Argentina	22
Panama	21
Costa Rica	17
Peru	15
Venezuela	11
Uruguay	9
Ecuador	9
Bolivia	8
Belize	6
Guyana	4
Haiti	4
Paraguay	3
Dominican Republic	2
The Bahamas	2
Barbados	1
Saint Kitts and Nevis	1
Puerto Rico	1

Source: Igarapé Institute, *Citizen Security Dashboard*.

Like security sector reform, citizen security is an evolving concept, and efforts are still underway to build evidence of its impacts on the ground.[157] While there is growing political support and rising investment, including from donor countries in North America and Western Europe, this will be difficult to sustain in the absence of clear outcome metrics of success.[158] There are also legitimate questions about the extent to which citizen security innovations can be replicated. Notwithstanding a wealth of scientific impact evaluations in North American and Western European settings, there are surprisingly few scientific impact evaluation studies in Latin America and the Caribbean.[159]

One effort to categorize citizen security measures captured some 1,300 discrete interventions across 26 countries between 1998 to 2015.[160] While the assessment is not exhaustive, it nevertheless facilitates the analysis of trends.[161] For one, it highlights just 85 impact evaluations, of which just 18 met basic scientific requirements. Notwithstanding the still limited evidence base, citizen security is widely considered a development priority across Latin America and the Caribbean, especially for mayors and municipal leaders.[162] It allows for the combination of a wide range of activities, from situational prevention and preventive policing to judicial and penal reform and social interventions.

The legacy of citizen security interventions is on balance positive. There are security and safety dividends arising from discrete interventions, though their scalability is routinely questioned. There are also potentially far-reaching impacts of citizen security on the security sector and wider democratic governance. Citizen security can and is reshaping security policies both domestically and intra-regionally. It also has the potential to challenge the militarization of police functions.[163] Even so, despite the spread of citizen security innovations across Brazil, Colombia and Mexico over the past decade, there is still persistent support for punitive and repressive approaches to fighting crime in Latin America.[164] Many governments still pursue policies favoring mass incarceration, emphasizing the importance of lowering the age of criminal responsibility, building prisons and stiffening penalties. There also continues to be a disproportionate focus on penalizing drug-related crimes, including possession and consumption, that has contributed to mass incarceration and over-crowding of prisons.

While there are hopeful signs of a shift to more citizen security oriented approaches, they need more support.[165] Their usefulness needs to be demonstrated on both empirical and cost-effectiveness grounds. Robust impact evaluations are critical, as are opportunities for Latin American and Caribbean policy makers to share experiences. Innovative financing mechanisms are also urgently required if the funding gaps are to be bridged. The financing gap is real. A recent study estimates that Latin American governments spent between US$55 and US$70 billion on conventional public security—police, justice and prisons—in 2014, with a much smaller proportion devoted to violence prevention measures and strategies to reintegrate former inmates.[166] There are also signs of significant reductions in spending from bilateral and multilateral partners over the past decade.[167]

Urban Citizen Security Experiences in Latin America and the Caribbean

Latin American and Caribbean cities have served as laboratories for innovative approaches to preventing and reducing crime and violence through a combination of public security and preventive measures. Part of this is due to shifts in national laws and norms in the 1980s and 1990s. Following military dictatorships across the region, new governments introduced constitutional and legislative changes that articulated, in some cases for the first time, a citizen's right to safety and security. They also introduced parallel reforms to the police, justice and prison services to safeguard this right.

As the concept of citizen security began to spread, municipalities emerged as the new center of democratic and administrative action. Municipalities also worked with newly created national interior and justice ministries to coordinate activities with law enforcement and criminal justice entities. Furthermore, new centers of expertise on crime prevention emerged—together with designated municipal secretariats, departments and commissions—to help design, monitor and evaluate interventions. City level citizen security efforts have generated remarkable successes across Latin America. Once notoriously violent cities, such as Bogota, San Pedro Sula, Sao Paulo and Medellin, have witnessed 70–90 per cent drops in murder rates over the past two decades.[168] While offering a glimpse of what is possible, these experiences are still rare. What is required is a comprehensive vision of citizen security that accounts for multiple levels of government and multi-sector interventions. These measures require reliable and high-quality data and analysis, developed in partnership with affected communities.

Citizen security encompasses a set of practices, measures and experiences that are still evolving.[169] While there have been well over a thousand interventions undertaken across Latin America since the late 1990s, only a comparatively small number of them have been subject to

How to cite this book chapter:
Muggah, R. and de Boer, J. 2019. *Security Sector Reform and Citizen Security: Experiences from Urban Latin America in Global Perspective.* Pp. 23–28. London: Ubiquity Press. DOI: https://doi.org/10.5334/bcc.f. License: CC-BY 4.0

scientific evaluation.[170] While there is growing investment by development banks, such as CAF and IADB, in funding experimental and quasi-experimental research[171], less than 7% of all documented interventions have any sort of robust assessment.[172] Even so, there are successful approaches to promoting citizen security that are strongly associated with positive outcomes and, while not directly applicable or replicable, offer opportunities for learning and even south-south cooperation.

Table 7. *A sample of citizen security measures in selected Latin American cities.*

	Name	**Mechanism**	**Funding**	**Approach**
Aguascalientes (2010–present)	Politica Publica de Convivencia y Seguridad Ciudadana	Master plan and facilitating mechanism (Convive Feliz)	Federal, municipal, national oil company (US$40 million)	A combination of urban renewal, outdoor recreation, youth programs
Bogota (1993–present)	Multiple interventions across several administrations	Master plans and a specialized sub-secretariat/ departments	Federal, municipal, international, private	A combination of civic education, municipal police reform, alcohol/ firearms regulation, urban renewal in key areas
Ciudad Juarez (2011–present)	Todos Somos Juarez	Special coordinating committee (Mesa de Seguranca) and citizen councils	Federal, state, municipal and private (US$400 million)	Community policing, school and university building, parks creation, targeted social welfare, credit and loan schemes, etc.
Montevideo (2012–present)	Programa Integral de Seguridad Ciudadana	Specialized crime prevention units, integrated crime mapping platform	Federal, municipal, international (US$15 million)	Problem-oriented and hot spot policing, urban design to improve safety, school outreach programs, recidivism reduction activities, programs focused on domestic violence
Rio de Janeiro (2008–2015)	Unidades de Polícia Pacificadora	Special Operations Battalion followed by public service provision	Federal and Municipal	A combination of proximity, community policing, with social programs that sought to integrate favelas into the rest of the community.
Medellin (2001–2009)	Social urbanism and urban acupuncture	Masterplan of integrated urban projects	Municipal	An integrated urban project that sought to improve relations between local administration and the national police forces by investing in improving public spaces in neighborhoods with the highest levels of poverty and crime that were equipped with public services.

What are the ingredients of success? While every situation is different, key ingredients include crafting a clear strategy with a determined focus on high-risk places, people and behaviors. A significant part of the solution requires addressing the specific risks: persistent inequality, youth unemployment, weak security and justice institutions and organized crime groups fueled by drug trafficking. There are also several practices, including focused deterrence strategies, cognitive therapy for at risk youth, early childhood and parenting support and targeted efforts to reduce concentrated poverty, with a positive track record.[173] This section considers a sample of experiences from Brazil, Colombia, Mexico and Uruguay.

Colombia is a leader in innovative citizen security programs. One of the most well-known national strategies is the *Plan Nacional de Vigilancia Comunitaria por Cuadrantes*, known as Plan Cuadrantes, initiated in 2010. It initially focused on eight of Colombia's largest cities: Bogota, Medellin, Cali, Barranquilla, Cartagena, Bucaramanga, Pereira and Cúcuta. Over a period of two years, more than 9,000 police were involved in community and problem-oriented policing strategies (including foot patrols) to address neighborhood-level challenges. Cities were divided into small areas (cuadrantes) with six officers per area. Impact evaluations registered a 22 per cent reduction in homicide, though rates varied from city to city.[174]

It is not just national initiatives but, even more importantly, individual city-driven initiatives that stand out. Starting in the 1990s, Cali mayor, Rodrigo Guerrero, pursued data-driven crime control with impressive results. In Bogota, a succession of mayors, beginning in 1997 with Antanas Mockus and later Enrique Peñalosa and Luis Eduardo Garzon, launched so-called 'citizen co-existence' and citizen security interventions with dramatic gains. Meanwhile, Medellin mayors Luis Perez and Sergio Fajardo introduced social urbanism together with principles of transparency and zero tolerance for corruption, and these strategies continued with mayors over the following decade.[175] Key to the success of these efforts were the sustained collection of data and hot spot policing, social welfare programs in high risk neighborhoods, a focus on ensuring high quality public goods in areas experiencing concentrated poverty and multi-sector interventions that stressed mobility, education, youth employment and inequality de-concentration.

Driven by a succession of committed mayors working in partnership with private and civic leaders, the results of these city-led crime prevention efforts are nothing short of breathtaking.[176] Take the case of Medellin, which in 1991 had a homicide rate of 381 per 100,000. Medellin's homicide rate in 2017 is closer to 21 per 100,000, far below that of many US cities.[177] Bogota's murder rate dropped from 80 per 100,000 in 1993 to 16 per 100,000 today. Even Cali and Barranquilla's stubbornly high rates have fallen to historic lows. This is good news considering these four cities account for one third of all murders in Colombia.

While the headlines are often pessimistic, Brazil is a laboratory of innovation when it comes to citizen security. There are many examples of innovative policing, criminal justice, penal and prevention programs across the country since the 1990s. Some are more widely known than others. They share some common features, including comprehensive approaches combining community policing with social and economic investment in marginal areas of concentrated poverty. They have also struggled with similar challenges, including changes in leadership and funding gaps and persistent inequality and uneven government support over the long term.

Consider the case of metropolitan Sao Paulo, which witnessed a dramatic reduction in its murder rate from 52.5 per 100,000 in 1999 to just 6.1 per 100,000 today.[178] Researchers attribute this drop to a combination of SSR-inspired institutional reforms, including not only police reform, but also citizen security related measures, including regulations related to gun control, alcohol restrictions and even a Pax Mafiosi by a major gang, the PCC. The most important interventions involved the deployment of community police units working in tough areas, new guidelines on the use of force, data-driven crime mapping tools (called Infocrim), rewards for good performance, human rights and technical training, improvements in investigation and better coordination between military and civil police forces.

Another program in Sao Paulo was launched in 2002 in the suburb of Diadema. Working with business and civil society groups, municipal authorities adopted controls on alcohol sales at night (closing down sales in hot spot areas after 11pm), monitored alcohol-selling vendors, installed public lighting and security cameras and introduced changes in public safety management procedures to strengthen police and municipal guard presence in hot spots. In the process, the city's homicide rate declined from 140 per 100,000 in 1997 to around 21 per 100,000 by 2008. Key to the program's early success was strong community buy-in, outreach to alcohol retailers, and persistent enforcement of the rules and penalties for non-compliance.

Meanwhile, in Rio de Janeiro, two programs are credited with generating reductions in lethal violence between 2009 and 2015. The first was a state-wide 'system of targets'[179] for military police, which set remunerated performance targets for incentivizing reductions in lethal and non-lethal crime. The second included pacification police units (UPP)[180] that enlisted more than 9,000 newly recruited officers, deploying them to 38 areas across the metropolitan capital.[181] Between 2009 and 2015, homicide rates dropped by 66 per cent, though they started creeping back up in 2016 in the wake of political scandal, economic crisis and collapsing leadership. In addition to failing to address systemic social and economic challenges, the intervention came under heavy criticism for a series of abuses committed by UPP police themselves.

Mexico has also invested intensively in citizen security at the city scale. Consider the case of Ciudad Juarez, a sprawling city of 1.3 million, which experienced a dramatic surge in criminal violence from 2008 to 2011, largely due to gang-related territorial violence and *mano dura* policies implemented by the Mexican government. The absolute number of homicides garnered global headlines, increasing by more than 700 per cent, from 192 (2008) to 1,589 (2009) to 3,766 (2010), reaching a homicide rate of 271 per 100,000. Extreme levels of violent crime effectively shut down the city: an estimated 37,000 businesses closed and a quarter of the population fled across the border to the US and other parts of Mexico. A number of factors shaped Ciudad Juarez's vulnerability to crime and victimization. A series of rolling protests from 2008 to 2009 set the stage for change.

Another program developed in partnership between municipal and federal governments in Mexico, *Todos Somos Juarez*, was formally launched in 2010. The US$400 million initiative 'drew inspiration from the Medellin experience.'[182] The objective was to mitigate risks for crime around six core sectors: public security, economic growth, employment, health, education and social development. The program spanned different levels of government, the private sector and civil society. It emphasized shifting internal security in the city away from armed forces and punitive law enforcement to an approach emphasizing 'social and economic prevention strategies.'[183] This included massive investment in urban renewal schemes—schools, universities and parks—as well as extending harm reduction, poverty reduction and credit and loan schemes to tens of thousands of families. Citizen councils were created to make decisions around investments, and with that, community engagement became a foundational principal of citizen security. Federal agencies were required to work closely with state and municipal counterparts, with weekly reports feeding back to the president's office.

While far from problem-free, *Todo Somos Juarez* is said to have contributed to a drop in the homicide rate from 271 to 19 per 100,000 between 2010 and 2015. Reports indicate that 'rates of school attendance also increased dramatically, and more people reclaimed the streets that had previously been barren.'[184] There were, however, criticisms of incomplete projects and unmet expectations. Sustaining progress has also been an issue as rates of violence climbed in recent years.

Another celebrated Mexican program was launched in Aguascalientes, a city of roughly 886,000 residents (in 2017) and one of Mexico's larger metropolitan areas. The mayor, Lorena Martinez, explored an environmental design strategy in 2010 to recover degraded areas of the city. The focus was on recovering a neglected zone with a catchment of roughly 300,000 people, with efforts to improve urban governance, encourage the use of public space, promote community participation and create sustainable measures to promote public security and local development.[185]

The municipal government assumed a lead role in designing and implementing a US$40 million dollar intervention known as *Linea Verde*. The area was inaccessible due to the presence of gas pipelines and rising drug-related violence. The first step was to develop a master plan involving physical and social measures to foster community cohesion, which were intended to eliminate opportunities for drug trafficking, provide areas for young people to gather and provide high quality infrastructure. [186] The program appears to be delivering results. According to the municipality, violent assault and robbery have declined by 50 per cent since it was launched.[187]

Meanwhile, another promising citizen security measure is underway in Montevideo, a city of 1.3 million people. Faced with increasing street crime, youth violence and domestic abuse, public authorities launched a series of crime prevention strategies that combine deterrence and community outreach.[188] The country has a long history extending back to the 1990s of initiating innovative crime prevention strategies. The latest—an integrated local management program for citizen security (2012–2015) and a new problem-oriented policing and community intervention initiative (2016–present)—are particularly interesting.

The Montevideo authorities initiated the 'integrated local management program for citizen security' as a pilot in 2012. This US$7 million dollar project was aimed at suppressing crime and strengthening social cohesion in three specific neighborhoods exhibiting high rates of crime.[189] The focus of the project was to 'improve the quality of the social support networks on the ground, strengthen statistics collection and evaluations of existing activities, improve human resource management' to help young people overcome drug dependency and 'leave the street.'[190]

Based on the results of the pilot, these efforts were scaled up in April 2016 with support from the IADB's Integrated Program for Citizen Security. At the center of the new US$8 million initiative is a problem-oriented policing initiative that is designed to improve operational and strategic policing at the neighborhood level. The program includes the training of some 1,100 police officers in problem-oriented policing (POP) to reduce robberies and build on a hot-spot policing program in Montevideo (Uruguay) called the *Program de Alta Dedicación Operativo* (PADO).[191]

Complementing PADO is the *Pelota al Medio al la Esperanza* program, which includes a range of activities designed to promote co-existence and mitigate the risks of crime and violence. The program concentrates investments in hot-spot neighborhoods. These investments include employment schemes for former inmates, educational programs, open urban spaces and micro-level projects. The overall goal is to 'help promote underlying social cohesion and efficacy to diminish the risk of inter-personal and intimate partner victimization.'[192] The initiative was evaluated by IADB as having contributed to considerable impact, including a 22 per cent decline in robbery in areas where it was deployed. In some areas, robbery dropped by more than 60 per cent.[193]

It is worth noting that many public authorities across Latin America, including in Colombia, Brazil, El Salvador and Mexico, have resorted to informal pacts and truces with organized crime groups to reduce crime and violence. The evidence suggests that such informal agreements are seldom effective in the medium- to long-term.[194] They can generate short-term reductions in homicide, but when they collapse, as they often do, levels of criminal violence can return to (or exceed) levels seen before the agreement. The problem seems to be one of credibility: in the absence of predictable rules and third-party enforcement, repeat gains become more difficult. Truces and pacts with cartels and gangs are also exceedingly unpopular with the public.[195] In post-war settings, ceasefires and peace agreements have clear confidence-building and verification measures, usually backed by a credible third party. Similar guarantees rarely, if ever, exist outside war zones and could give rise to moral hazards, including impunity, extortion and corruption at the local level.

The aforementioned examples from Brazil, Colombia, Mexico and Uruguay are far from the only innovative citizen security measures introduced by cities. The *Barrio Seguro* program in

Santo Domingo (Dominican Republic) is 'credited with rebuilding trust in crime-affected neighborhoods and reducing murder rates.'[196] The program has been scaled from 2 to 13 neighborhoods since it was launched. Quito (Ecuador) has also actively sought to improve community policing by linking citizens with police through mobile phones, and the impact has been an improved sense of safety and responsiveness.

City-based programs often adapt, borrow and gain inspiration from multiple locations. The best ideas are often those that have a positive track record. Virtually all of the most successful programs are amalgams of previous ones. Take the case of Linea Verde, which borrowed directly from experiences in Curitiba and Medellin. Or consider the case of Montevideo, which drew insights from Bogota and London. Meanwhile, Bogota drew its inspiration from Spain, while Medellin learned lessons from Bogota and New York. Mayors are pragmatic and action-oriented, and there is no reason why good ideas cannot be adapted and replicated to positive effect.

Emerging Insights for Adopting a Citizen Security Lens to SSR

Lessons from Latin America point to the notion that cities, and in particular mayors and other civic leaders, are assuming an increasingly central role in shaping SSR and citizen security. This shift started in the 1990s and 2000s, particularly with cities like Bogota and Montevideo, and often with support from institutions, such as the Inter-American Development Bank, among others. Over time, some city experiences acquired more notoriety than others. For example, interventions launched in Ciudad Juarez, Medellin and Rio de Janeiro have spawned a cottage industry of research. There are many others, including those highlighted in this paper, such as Aguascalientes, that received comparatively less attention.[197] These cities introduced a host of approaches, including those borrowed from other countries, such as problem-oriented policing and more indigenous experimentations with urban acupuncture and social urbanism. Together, these approaches provide a number of important insights on how SSR and citizen security can combine to improve the accountability, effectiveness and transparency of security and justice sector institutions in urban contexts.

First, the very nature and variety of violence being experienced in Latin American cities requires close coordination between bottom-up and top-down efforts, as well as formal and informal approaches to security. When it comes to high intensity organized crime, there may be more involvement of federal-level institutions and intelligence-led operations, where SSR focuses on institutional capacity building and increased effectiveness is a priority. With respect to lower-intensity street crime and domestic violence, the strategies tend to be more balanced and citizen oriented. Here citizen security approaches may be most appropriate as they combine both deterrence and prevention. Ultimately, any strategy must be informed by context; a careful sequencing

How to cite this book chapter:
Muggah, R. and de Boer, J. 2019. *Security Sector Reform and Citizen Security: Experiences from Urban Latin America in Global Perspective*. Pp. 29–30. London: Ubiquity Press. DOI: https://doi.org/10.5334/bcc.g. License: CC-BY 4.0

of SSR and citizen security oriented approaches based on contextual characteristics will enhance the effectiveness of interventions.

Second, across virtually all settings, a diverse array of structural, institutional and proximate risk factors give rise to crime and victimization. These factors can range from the availability and abuse of alcohol to the availability of firearms and the abundance of drug trafficking networks, as well as systemic corruption and widespread inequality. Citizen security helps SSR move beyond a narrow focus on the form and function of formal and informal security institutions and account for the rights of individuals, together with a more comprehensive set of factors and measures to improve safety and well-being. Ultimately, interventions at the city level must be selective in their approaches and seek to address crime and violence based on a careful diagnostic of the particular factors that exacerbate insecurity in their context, particularly in contexts where a multiplicity of actors (i.e.. militias, community self-defence forces, private security companies, paramilitary groups and gangs) shape security dynamics on the ground. Lessons from Latin America indicate that strategies that carefully map out key risks, communicate priorities, marshal resources from multiple sources and develop coordinated strategies across multiple layers of government, business and civil society are most successful.

Finally, communities must be engaged in the design, implementation, evaluation and communication of security strategies. All successful interventions reveal that the process matters. Affected communities need to feel that they are owners of the process if interventions are to be considered legitimate or if social cohesion is to be fostered. Citizen security measures that actively canvass public opinion, that involve multiple stakeholders in the preparation of diagnostics and action plans and that regularly provide evidence of results are likely to outlast initiatives that do not. Such efforts are central to building the trust and confidence in security and justice institutions, which is also a core objective of SSR.

Endnotes

1. See Schroeder, U.C. and Chappuis. F (2014). "New Perspectives on Security Sector Reform: The Role of Local Agency and Domestic Politics", International Peacekeeping, 21:2, p. 135. DOI: https://doi.org/10.1080/13533312.2014.910401.

2. See OECD DAC (2007). "Handbook on Security System Reform: Supporting Security and Justice", Paris. https://www.eda.admin.ch/dam/deza/en/documents/themen/fragile-kontexte/224402-oecd-handbook-security-system-reform_EN.pdf.

3. See UN Security Council Resolution S/RES/2151 (2014) http://unscr.com/files/2014/02151.pdf.

4. See UN-World Bank Group (2017). "Pathways for Peace: Inclusive Approaches to Preventing Violent Conflict", Washington D.C.

5. See Jackson, P. (2018). "Introduction: Second-Generation Security Sector Reform", Journal of Intervention and Statebuilding, 12:1, 1–10, DOI: https://doi.org/10.1080/17502977.2018.1426384.

6. See Schroeder and Chappuis (2014). op cit.

7. See Sedra, M. (2015). "Transitioning from first to second generation security sector reform in conflict-affected countries", ed. Paul Jackson Handbook of International Security and Development, Edward Elgar (Cheltenham UK). Also see Detzner, S. (2017). "Modern post-conflict security sector reform in Africa: patterns of success and failure", African Security Review, 26:2, 116–142, DOI: https://doi.org/10.1080/10246029.2017.1302706.

8. See Jackson, P. (2018) op cit. Also see Detzner, S. (2017). "Modern post-conflict security sector reform in Africa: Patterns of success and failure, African Security Review", 26:2, 116–142, DOI: https://doi.org/10.1080/10246029.2017.1302706. Also see Proksik, J. (2013) "Organized Crime and the Dilemmas of Democratic Peace-Building in Kosovo", International Peacekeeping, Vol.20, No.3, pp.280–298.

9. See Jackson P. (2017). "Capacity Building and Security Sector Reform", in: Dover R., Dylan H., Goodman M. (eds) The Palgrave Handbook of Security, Risk and Intelligence. Palgrave Macmillan, London.

10. Albrecht, P. and Wiuff, (2015). "The simultaneity of authority in hybrid orders", Peacebuilding 3(1): 1–16. DOI: https://doi.org/10.1080/21647259.2014.928551. See Detzner (2017) op cit. Also see DCAF (2018) "Examining the Urban Dimensions of the Security Sector",

https://www.dcaf.ch/sites/default/files/publications/documents/Examiningper cent20theper cent20Urbanper cent20Dimensionper cent20ofper cent20theper cent20Securityper cent20 Sector_18Feb2018.pdf. Price, M. and Warren, M. (2017). "Reimagining SSR in Contexts of Security Pluralism", Stability: International Journal of Security and Development, 6 (1), p.8. DOI: http://doi.org/10.5334/sta.555.

[11] Muggah, R. (2018a) "The Rise of Citizen Security in Latin America and the Caribbean", International Development Policy 10 (1): 291–322. https://journals.openedition.org/poldev/2377.

[12] See Flom, H. (2018) "The Political Economy of Citizen Security: A Conceptual Framework", IADB, August. https://publications.iadb.org/bitstream/handle/11319/9110/The-Political-Economy-of-Citizen-Security-A-Conceptual-Framework.pdf?sequence=1&isAllowed=y.

[13] See OECD DAC, (2007). op cit.

[14] For a list of case studies covering these cases see ISSAT's case study library: https://issat.dcaf.ch/esl/Learn/Resource-Library/Case-Studies.

[15] Muggah, R. and Sullivan, J. (2018). "The Coming Crime Wars", Foreign Policy, 21 September, https://foreignpolicy.com/2018/09/21/the-coming-crime-wars/.

[16] Piche, G. R. (2016). "Assessing the Impact of Orthodox Security Sector Reform in El Salvador", CSG Paper n. 10. Centre for Security Governance https://issat.dcaf.ch/Learn/Resource-Library2/Policy-and-Research-Papers/Assessing-the-Impact-of-Orthodox-Security-Sector-Reform-in-El-Salvador. Also see ISSAT (2017). "Honduras SSR Background Note", Geneva Centre for Security Sector Governance (https://issat.dcaf.ch/Learn/Resource-Library2/Country-Profiles/Honduras-SSR-Background-Note); also see Muggah. R. (March 2016). "The State of Security and Justice in Brazil: Reviewing the Evidence", Elliott School of International Affairs. https://igarape.org.br/wp-content/uploads/2016/04/The-State-of-Security-and-Justice-in-Brazil-Reviewing-the-Evidence.pdf.

[17] Gavigan, P. (2009). "Organized Crime, Illicit Power Structures and Guatemala's Threatened Peace Process", International Peacekeeping, Vol.16, No.1, pp.62–76.

[18] Muggah, R. and Sullivan, J. (2018) "The Coming Crime Wars", Foreign Policy, 21 September, https://foreignpolicy.com/2018/09/21/the-coming-crime-wars/.

[19] de Boer, J. and Bosetti, L. (2015). "The Crime-Conflict 'Nexus': State of the Evidence", UNU-CPR (https://i.unu.edu/media/cpr.unu.edu/attachment/1665/OC_05-The-Crime-Conflict-Nexus.pdf).

[20] See Sharkey, P (2018). Uneasy Peace: The Great Crime Decline, the Renewal of City Life and the New War on Violence, New York: New York University Press. For an excellent review of the book seek Gopnik, A. (2018). "The Great Crime Decline: Drawing the right lessons from the fall in urban violence." The New Yorker (Available at: https://www.newyorker.com/magazine/2018/02/12/the-great-crime-decline).

[21] Bergman, M. (2018). More Money, More Crime: Prosperity and Rising Crime in Latin America. Oxford University Press, Oxford, UK.

[22] See Muggah, R. (2004) "Changing the Drug Policy Narrative", OpenCanada, 8 September, https://www.opencanada.org/features/changing-the-drug-policy-narrative/.

[23] See Muggah, R. and Garzon, J. (2018b). "La Mano Dura: Los Costos de la Represion y los Beneficios de la Prevencion para los Jovenes en America Latina", Strategic Paper 36, Igarapé Institute, https://igarape.org.br/wp-content/uploads/2018/06/La-Mano-Dura-Los-costos-de-la-represioper centCCper cent81n-y-los-beneficios-de-la-prevencioper centCCper cent81n-para-los-joper centCCper cent81venes-en-Ameper centCCper cent81rica-Latina.pdf.

[24] See Muggah, R. (2018c). "Reviewing the Costs and Benefits of Mano Dura vs Crime Prevention in the Americas", in Shaw, T. et al (eds), The Palgrave Handbook of Contemporary International Political Economy. Oxford: Palgrave.

[25] See Muggah, R. and Alvarado, N. (2018). "Crimen y Violencia: Un Obstaculo Para el Desarrollo de las Ciudades de America Latina y Caribe", IADB 644, https://publications.iadb.org/bitstream/

handle/11319/9340/Crimen-y-violencia-un-obstaculo-para-el-desarrollo-de-las-ciudades-de-America-Latina-y-el-Caribe-final.pdf?sequence=1&isAllowed=y.

26 See Muggah, R. et al (2016). "Making Cities Safer: Citizen Security Innovations from Latin America", Strategic Paper 20, IADB and World Economic Forum and Igarapé Institute, https:// publications.iadb.org/handle/11319/7757.

27 See Ibid and Muggah (2018). op cit.

28 Levels of urbanization vary. In Argentina, Brazil and Chile between 85–91per cent of the populations are urban, while in Ecuador, El Salvador, Mexico and Peru the rates vary from 63–76 per cent.

29 See Muggah, R. (2018) "There´s a Cure for Latin America´s Murder Epidemic – and it Doesn´t Involve More Police or Prisons", Agenda, 2017, https://www.weforum.org/agenda/2017/04/ there-s-a-cure-for-latin-america-s-murder-epidemic-and-it-doesn-t-involve-more-police-or-prisons/.

30 See Aguirre, K. and Muggah, R. (2018d) Citizen Security in Latin America: Facts and Figures, Strategic Paper 33, CAF and Igarapé Institute, https://igarape.org.br/wp-content/ uploads/2018/04/Citizen-Security-in-Latin-America-Facts-and-Figures.pdf.

31 Muggah, R (2017) "How to Fix Latin America´s Homicide Problem", The Conversation, June 28, https://theconversation.com/how-to-fix-latin-americas-homicide-problem and Muggah, (2017) "Latin America´s Murder Epidemic", Foreign Affairs, https://www.foreignaffairs.com/ articles/central-america-caribbean/2017-03-22/latin-americas-murder-epidemic.

32 See the special collection of essays on citizen security in the Stabilization Journal available at https://www.stabilityjournal.org/collections/special/citizen-security-dialogues-making-brazilian-cities-safer/.

33 Muggah (2018). op cit.

34 Muggah, R. and Szabo, I. (2014). "Changes in the Neighborhood: Reviewing Citizen Security Cooperation in Latin America", Strategic Paper 7, Igarapé Institute, https://igarape.org.br/ wp-content/uploads/2014/03/AE-07-Changes-in-the-Neighborhood_10th_march.pdf.

35 Ibid.

36 Luckham, R. (2017). "Whose violence, whose security? Can violence reduction and security work for poor, excluded and vulnerable people?" Peacebuilding, 5:2, 99–117, DOI: https:// doi.org/10.1080/21647259.2016.1277009.

37 See UNDP (2013/2014). Citizen Security With a Human Face. New York: UNDP, http://hdr. undp.org/en/content/citizen-security-human-face.

38 See Sedra (2015).

39 See OECD (2007).

40 See https://issat.dcaf.ch/Share/People-and-Organisations/Organisations/United-Nations-SSR-Inter-Agency-Task-Force.

41 Jackson (2018). p. 1. Also see Schroeder and Chappuis (2014).

42 See Sedra (2018).

43 See Sedra (2015); Schroeder and Chappuis (2014); Jackson (2018); Detzner (2017).

44 See OECD (2008).

45 Olonisakin, F. and Bryden A. (2010). "Security Sector Transformation in Africa." DCAF. LIT Verlag. https://www.dcaf.ch/sites/default/files/publications/documents/Yearlyper cent2520Book.pdf.

46 See Jackson (2018).

47 World Bank (2011). "World Development Report" Washington D.C. UN High Level Panel on Peace Operations (2015), "Uniting our strengths for peace – politics, partnerships and people", New York. https://peaceoperationsreview.org/wp-content/uploads/2015/08/HIPPO_Report_1_ June_2015.pdf; and UN and World Bank (2018) op cit. https://www.worldbank.org/en/topic/ fragilityconflictviolence/publication/pathways-for-peace-inclusive-approaches-to-preventing-violent-conflict.

48 Detzner (2017).

49 Schroeder and Chappuis (2014), Detzner (2017).

50 Schroeder and Chappuis (2014).

51 Muggah, R. (2015). "Fixing Fragile Cities", Foreign Affairs, January, https://www.foreignaffairs.com/articles/africa/2015-01-15/fixing-fragile-cities and de Boer, J. et al (2016). "Peacekeeping in Cities: Is the UN Prepared?", United Nations University, Centre for Policy Research, Tokyo, Japan. (Available at: https://cpr.unu.edu/peacekeeping-in-cities-is-the-un-prepared.html#1).

52 See OECD (2018). "Sates of Fragility", Paris. http://www.oecd.org/dac/states-of-fragility-2018-9789264302075-en.htm.

53 UN Habitat (2017). "The New Urban Agenda", (p. 27) http://habitat3.org/wp-content/uploads/NUA-English.pdf,. Also see OECD (2016), "States of Fragility 2016" Paris. http://www.oecd.org/dac/states-of-fragility-2016-9789264267213-en.htm.

54 Muggah, R. (2015). "A Manifesto for the Fragile City", Journal of International Affairs, 68 (2), http://gsdrc.org/wp-content/uploads/2016/07/fragile-cities-muggah-2015-columbia-journal.pdf and de Boer, J. and Muggah, R. (2015). "The Sustainable Development fight will be won or lost in our cities", World Economic Forum: The Agenda. https://www.weforum.org/agenda/2015/09/the-fight-for-sustainable-development-will-be-won-or-lost-in-our-cities/.

55 DCAF (2018). "Examining the Urban Dimensions of the Security Sector", Geneva. https://www.dcaf.ch/sites/default/files/publications/documents/Examiningper cent20theper cent20Urbanper cent20Dimensionper cent20ofper cent20theper cent20Securityper cent20Sector_18Feb2018.pdf.

56 See https://igarape.org.br/en/apps/citizen-security-dashboard/ for a review of over 1,200 citizen security measures between 1998 and 2018 in Latin America and the Caribbean.

57 Muggah, R. and Aguirre Tobón, K. (2018).

58 The average across Latin America is 21.5 per 100,000 people versus 7 per 100,000 for the rest of the world. See Muggah and Aguirre Tobón, op cit., p. 2. For data on Brazil see Seguranca Publica em Numeros 2018 (http://www.forumseguranca.org.br/wp-content/uploads/2018/08/FBSP_Anuario_Brasileiro_Seguranca_Publica_Infogrper centC3per centA1fico_2018.pdf).

59 Ibid.

60 Ibid.

61 See, for example, Muggah, R. and Aguirre, K. (2018) Citizen Security in Latin America: Facts and Figures, Strategic Paper 33, April, https://igarape.org.br/wp-content/uploads/2018/04/Citizen-Security-in-Latin-America-Facts-and-Figures.pdf; and Latinobarometro, Informe (2016) (https://imco.org.mx/politica_buen_gobierno/informe-latinobarometro-2016-via-latinobarometro/).

62 Muggah, R. and Aguirre, K. (2018) "Which Latin American Countries Got Safer in 2017?", Americas Quarterly, February 5, https://www.americasquarterly.org/content/which-latin-american-countries-got-safer-2017.

63 See for instance IDRC (2018). "Understanding and Estimating Displacement in the Northern Triangle of Central America", http://www.internal-displacement.org/publications/understanding-and-estimating-displacement-in-the-northern-triangle-of-central-america. For commentary on recent declines see The Economist (8 December 2018). "The Northern Triangle is Becoming Less Murderous." (https://www.economist.com/the-americas/2018/12/08/the-northern-triangle-is-becoming-less-murderous).

64 See Wilson Center (2018). "The Hidden Problem of Forced Internal Displacement in Central America." Washington D.C. https://www.wilsoncenter.org/article/the-hidden-problem-forced-internal-displacement-central-america.

65 See UNODC (2016) op cit.

66 See Jaitman, L., D. Caprirola, R. Granguillhome, P. Keefer, T. Leggett, J. Lewis, J. Mejia-Guerra, M. Mello, H. Sutton y I. Torre (2017). The Costs of Crime and Violence: New Evidence and Insights in Latin America and the Caribbean (Washington, D.C.: BID).

[67] Ibid.

[68] Specific clusters of countries are driving the high costs in each sub-region. In Central America, the high expenditure on private security is shaped by El Salvador and Honduras. In the Andean region, Colombia is the key driver, while in South America, it is Brazil and Venezuela that are driving up expenditures.
See Jaitman et al. (2017) op cit.

[69] The heads of State and Government of the Community of Latin American and Caribbean States (CELAC) declared the region as a 'zone of peace' in 2014. See http://celac.cubaminrex. cu/articulos/proclamation-latin-america-and-caribbean-zone-peace. See also Abdenur, A., Mattheis, F. and P. Seabra (2016) "An Ocean for the Global South: Brazil and the Zone of Peace and Cooperation in the South Atlantic", Cambridge Review of International Affairs 29 (3).

[70] See Muggah, R. and Abdenur, A. (2017) "How to Avoid a Venezuelan Civil War", Foreign Affairs, August, https://www.foreignaffairs.com/articles/venezuela/2017-08-09/how-avoid-venezuelan-civil-war, and Muggah, R. and Abdenur, A. (2019) "Brazil and Venezuela Clash Over Migrants, Humanitarian Aid and Closed Borders", the Conversation, 10 March, https://www.salon.com/2019/03/10/brazil-and-venezuela-clash-over-migrants-humanitarian-aid-and-closed-borders_partner/.

[71] Guarantor states in the case of Colombia included Norway and Cuba. Their role was to support and facilitate the peace process. See Nylander, D. and Sandberg. R. (2018). "Designing peace: The Colombian peace process." NOREF https://noref.no/Publications/Regions/Colombia/Designing-peace-the-Colombian-peace-process.

[72] Two cities are located in North America (United States) and seven in Africa (six in South Africa and one in Leshoto). See The Economist (April 2018). "Shining a Light on Latin America's Homicide Epidemic", https://www.economist.com/briefing/2018/04/05/shining-light-on-latin-americas-homicide-epidemic and The Economist (March 2017). "The World's Most Dangerous Cities", https://www.economist.com/graphic-detail/2017/03/31/the-worlds-most-dangerous-cities.

[73] See Aguirre, K. and Muggah, R. (2018) op cit.

[74] See Brotherton, D. and Gude, R. (2018) "Social Inclusion from Below: The Perspectives of Street Gangs and their Possible Effects on Declining Homicide Rates in Ecuador", IADB. Washington DC: IADB. See also Muggah, R. (2018) "Violent Crime in Sao Paulo has Dropped Dramatically. Is This Why?", Agenda, May 7, https://www.weforum.org/agenda/2018/03/violent-crime-in-sao-paulo-has-dropped-dramatically-this-may-be-why/.

[75] See Muggah, R. and Aguirre, K. (2018). "Reducing Latin America´s Hotspots", Journal of Aggression and Violent Behavior, https://app.dimensions.ai/details/publication/pub.1107398210?and_facet_journal=jour.1115384.

[76] See Muggah, R., Aguirre, K. and S. Chainey (2017). "Targeting Hot Spots Could Drastically Reduce Latin America´s Murder Rate", Americas Quarterly, 14 March, http://americasquarterly. org/content/targeting-hot-spots-could-drastically-reduce-latin-americas-murder-rate.

[77] U.S. studies have demonstrated that up to half of all crimes can be focused within 1 per cent of city blocks and 70 per cent of all crimes within 5 per cent. The same trend is seen in Latin America.

[78] See Mejia, D., Ortega, D., and K. Ortiz (2014). "Un analisis de la criminalidad urbana en Colombia", Background Paper for Igarapé Institute, https://igarape.org.br/wp-content/uploads/2015/01/Criminalidad-urbana-en-Colombia-diciembre-2014.pdf.

[79] See Chainey, S. and Muggah, R. (2019 forthcoming) "The micro-place concentration and near repeat victimisation of homicides in a Latin American urban context", Journal of Homicide Studies (under review).

[80] See Caumartin C., Molina G., Thorp R. (2008). "Inequality, Ethnicity and Political Violence in Latin America: The Cases of Bolivia, Guatemala and Peru", in: Stewart F. (eds) Horizontal Inequalities and Conflict. Conflict, Inequality and Ethnicity. Palgrave Macmillan, London;

Human Rights Watch (2017) "Bolivia: Events of 2017", New York: HRW, https://www.hrw.org/world-report/2018/country-chapters/bolivia and TeleSur (2016) "Paramiltiaries in Mexico Silencing Indigenous Community", TeleSur, 8 January, https://www.telesurtv.net/english/news/Paramilitaries-in-Mexico-Silencing-Indigenous-Community--20160108-0021.html.

[81] See Morrison, J. (2015) "Behind the Numbers: Race and Ethnicity in Latin America", Americas Quarterly, Summer Edition, http://www.americasquarterly.org/content/behind-numbers-race-and-ethnicity-latin-america.

[82] See United Nations (2014). "Elimination and Responses to Violence, Exploitation, and Abuse of Indigenous Girls, Adolescents and Young Women." Inter-Agency Support Group on Indigenous People´s Issues. http://www.un.org/en/ga/president/68/pdf/wcip/IASGper cent20Thematicper cent20Paper_per cent20Violenceper cent20againstper cent20Girlsper cent20andper cent20Womenper cent20-per cent20rev1.pdf.

[83] Rates are particularly high in Central America: El Salvador (349/100,000 women), Honduras (466/100,000 women) and Guatemala (211/100,000 women), but are also high in countries that otherwise have relatively low overall homicide rates. This includes Argentina (254/100,000 women), Bolivia (104/100,000 women) and Peru (100/100,000 women).

[84] See Ackerman, V. and T. Murray (2004). "Assessing Spatial Patterns of Crime in Lima, Ohio." Cities, 21(5), pp. 423–437.

[85] See Vilalta, C. and Muggah, R. (2014). "Violent Disorder in Ciudad Juaréz: A Spatial Analysis of Homicide", Trends in Organized Crime 17(3), pp. 161–180, DOI: https://doi.org/10.1007/s12117-014-9213-0.

[86] See Vilalto and Muggah (2014), op. cit. and Krivo, L. and R. Peterson (1996) "Extremely Disadvantaged Neighborhoods and Urban Crime", Social Forces, 75 (2), pp. 619–648.

[87] See Florida. R. (August 2018), "The Geography of Urban Violence" City Lab https://www.citylab.com/life/2018/08/the-geography-of-urban-violence/567928/. Also see Patrick Sharkey's data visualization on violence in America https://www.citylab.com/life/2018/08/the-geography-of-urban-violence/567928/.

[88] Salahub, J., Gottsbacher, M. and de Boer, J. (2018). Social Theories of Urban Violence in the Global South: Towards Safe and Inclusive Cities. London, Routeledge. https://idl-bnc-idrc.dspacedirect.org/bitstream/handle/10625/56926/IDL-56926.pdf.

[89] de Boer, J., Muggah, R. and Patel, R. (2016). "Conceptualizing City Resilience and Fragility." United Nations University, Centre for Policy Research, Tokyo, Japan. https://cpr.unu.edu/conceptualizing-city-fragility-and-resilience.html.

[90] See Soares, R. and J. Naritomi (2010). "Understanding High Crime Rates in Latin America. The Role of Social and Policy Factors", in R. Di Tella, S. Edwards and E. Schargrodsky (eds.) The Economics of Crime: Lessons for and from Latin America, 101 32 (Chicago: University of Chicago Press), http://www.nber.org/chapters/c11831.pdf.

[91] Intentional homicide typically does not include 'extra-judicial' or 'auto-defense' killings perpetrated by police, which tend to be captured under separate categories (if at all).

[92] See Muggah, R. (2015) "Latin America´s Poverty is Down, but Violence is Up. Why?", Americas Quarterly, 20 October, http://www.americasquarterly.org/content/latin-americas-poverty-down-violence-why.

[93] Ibid.

[94] See Salavitz, M. (2017) "The Surprising Factors Driving Murder Rates: Income Inequality and Respect", Guardian, 8 December, https://www.theguardian.com/us-news/2017/dec/08/income-inequality-murder-homicide-rates; Daly, M. (2016). Killing the Competition. Vancouver: UBC Press.

[95] See Glaeser. E., Resseger, M., and Tobio, K. (2009). "Inequalities in Cities." Journal of Regional Science, Vol. 49, No. 4, 2009, pp. 617-646. available at http://scholar.harvard.edu/files/resseger/

files/glaeserressegertobiojrs.pdf. Arguing that the link between income inequality and homicide was 'mixed', Aki Roberts and Dale Willits assessed income inequality measures against homicide in 208 large US cities and concluded that the two were correlated highly regardless of what measures of inequality one used. See Roberts A. and Willits, D. (2015).

[96] Consult http://www.worldbank.org/en/topic/poverty/lac-equity-lab1/overview.

[97] See Deas, M. and F. Daza (1995). "Dos Ensayos Especulativos Sobre la Violencia en Colombia", Bogota: Fonade and Fainzylber, P., D. Ledreman, and N. Loayza (2002). "What Causes Violent Crime?", European Economic Review 46, pp. 1323–1357.

[98] See World Bank (2018). "Wage Inequality in Latin America: Understanding the Past to Prepare for the Future." Washington DC: World Bank, https://openknowledge.worldbank.org/handle/10986/28682.

[99] According to some researchers, non-income measures of poverty, including infant mortality rates and limited social protection services, also seem to play a statistically significant role in shaping the trajectory of homicidal violence. See Pridemore, A.W. (2011). "Poverty Matters: A Reassessment of the Inequality-Homicide Relationship in Cross-National Studies", British Journal of Criminology, 51(1), pp. 739–772.

[100] See ILO (2017), "Annual Labour Overview of Latin America and the Caribbean", (https://www.ilo.org/global/about-the-ilo/newsroom/news/WCMS_614165/lang--en/index.htm).

[101] See Cerqueira and Moura (2015) op cit.

[102] See for example Raphael, S. and Winter-Ebmer, R. (2010). "Identifying the Effect of Unemployment on Crime", CEPR Discussion Paper 2299. Also see Carmichael. F., and Ward, R. (2001). "Male unemployment and crime in England and Wales," Economics Letters, 73(1) pp. 111–115 and Baron, S.W. (2008). "Street Youth, Unemployment, and Crime: Is It That Simple? Using General Strain Theory to Untangle the Relationship", Canadian Journal of Criminology and Criminal Justice, 50(4): 399 http://dx.doi.org/10.3138/cjccj.50.4.399.

[103] See Small Arms Survey (2016) More Women than Men Killed in Some High-Income Countries – New Study. Press release, http://www.smallarmssurvey.org/about-us/highlights/2016/highlight-rn63.html.

[104] See Pan American Health Organization and Centers for Disease Control and Prevention (2012). "Violence Against Women in Latin America and the Caribbean: A comparative analysis of population-based data from 12 countries", Washington, D.C. http://www1.paho.org/hq/dmdocuments/violence-against-women-lac.pdf.

[105] See Jewkes, R. (2002). "Intimate Partner Violence: Causes and Prevention," The Lancet. Vol. 359. pp. 1423–1429.

[106] See UNDP (2013). "Regional Human Development Report 2013/2014: Citizen Security with a Human Face", (New York: UNDP) http://hdr.undp.org/sites/default/files/citizen_security_with_a_human_face_-executivesummary.pdf.

[107] See UNODC (2016), op cit.

[108] See ICG (International Crisis Group) (2016). "Guatemala: Young Blood, Old Vices", 14 November, https://www.crisisgroup.org/latin-america-caribbean/central-america/guatemala/guatemala-young-blood-old-vices (Accessed 20 December 2016).

[109] See United Nations Office on Drugs and Crime (2018). "World Drug Report 2018", Vienna: UNODC, https://www.unodc.org/wdr2018/index.html.

[110] See Bergman, M. (2018). More Money, More Crime: Prosperity and Rising Crime in Latin America. Oxford University Press, Oxford, UK.

[111] Barreto, B. (30 April 2018). "El presidente Jimmy Morales y su partido, acorralados por mas investigaciones de corrupcion." Univision Noticias (Available at: https://www.univision.com/noticias/america-latina/el-presidente-jimmy-morales-y-su-partido-acorralados-por-mas-investigaciones-de-corrupcion) Castaneda, J. G. (12 April 2018). Has Latin America's Crusade

Against Corruption Gone Too Far?, The New York Times. (Available at: https://www.nytimes.com/2018/04/12/opinion/latin-america-corruption.html).

[112]   Muggah and Aguirre Tobón, op cit., p. 11.

[113]   Ortega, D. (2016). "Effectiveness versus legitimacy: Use of force and police training in Latin America." The Brookings Institution, Washington D.C. https://www.brookings.edu/blog/up-front/2016/01/05/effectiveness-versus-legitimacy-use-of-force-and-police-training-in-latin-america/.

[114]   See Aguirre, K. and Muggah, R. (2018c) "Assessing Diversion in Latin America", ATT Monitor. New York: ATT, https://attmonitor.org/en/wp-content/uploads/2018/08/EN_ATT_Monitor_Report_2018_ONLINE.pdf and Muggah (2015), op cit.

[115]   It is important to note that the 2030 Sustainable Development Agenda goal 16 seeks to address this very problem by getting countries to commit to significantly reducing the trafficking of illicit arms, combating corruption and developing transparent and accountable institutions. Also see Aguirre and Muggah (2018a) and Muggah, R. and Dudley (2016) "The Latin American Gun Leak", Los Angeles Times, 16 January, http://www.latimes.com/opinion/op-ed/la-oe-muggah-arming-latin-america-20150118-story.html.

[116]   See LAPOP (2017). "Beneath the Violence", Rule of Law Working Paper. (October). https://www.thedialogue.org/wp-content/uploads/2017/10/Crime-Avoidance-Report-FINAL-ONLINE.pdf/ and Muggah, R. and Winter, B. (2017) "Is Populism Making a Comeback in Latin America", Foreign Policy, October 23, http://foreignpolicy.com/2017/10/23/populism-is-coming-for-latin-america-in-2018/.

[117]   See Muggah and Winter (2017), op. cit.

[118]   Muggah, R., Garzón, J. C., and Suárez, M. (2018). "Mano Dura: The costs and benefits of re-pressive criminal justice for young people in Latin America", Igarape Institute (Available at: https://www.youth4peace.info/system/files/2018-04/1.per cent20TP_Manoper cent20Dura_Robper cent20Muggah.pdf).

[119]   The majority in the following countries support a *mano dura* approach: Costa Rica, 78 per cent; Panama and Peru, 77 per cent; Chile 75 per cent; Honduras and El Salvador, 73 per cent; Uruguay, 71 per cent and Guatemala, 63 per cent). See Latinobarometro, Informe 2016 (https://imco.org.mx/politica_buen_gobierno/informe-latinobarometro-2016-via-latinobarometro/).

[120]   United Nations Human Rights Council (2018). "Report of the Special Rapporteur on extrajudicial, summary or arbitrary executions on her mission to El Salvador." Thirty-eighth session https://www.ohchr.org/en/issues/executions/pages/srexecutionsindex.aspx.

[121]   Latinobarómetro (2018) Informe 2018. Baco de datos en linea.

[122]   According to 'broken windows' theory, petty crimes, intimidation and physical deterioration are the principle causes of crime because they scare off law-abiding citizens and allow delinquency to take root in a given area. 'Broken windows' suggests police can make areas safer by cracking down on minor 'quality-of-life' offenses, like vandalism or panhandling, on the assumption that strict enforcement of the law against petty crime will prevent more serious crime from taking root. See Kelling, G. and Wilson, J. (1982). "Broken windows: The police and neighborhood safety", Atlantic Monthly, Mar 249 (3): 29–38; and Ungar, M. and E. Arias (2012). "Community Policing in Latin America: Innovations and Challenges", Policing and Society, 22(1), http://www.tandfonline.com/toc/gpas20/22/1.

[123]   See https://cebcp.org/evidence-based-policing/what-works-in-policing/research-evidence-review/broken-windows-policing/.

[124]   See Ungar and Arias (2012), op. cit.

[125]   See Latinbarómeter (2018) and Cruz J. (2009) "Police Abuse in Latin America. Americas Barometer Insights 2009", Vanderbilt University, LAPOP, USAID.

[126]   See Cano, I. and Rojido, E. (2016) Mapping of Homicide Prevention Programs in Latin America and the Caribbean. Rio de Janeiro: UERJ.

[127] See Osse, A., and Cano, I. (2017) "Police deadly use of firearms: An international comparison", The International Journal of Human Rights, Taylor & Francis Group.

[128] CIDH (2018). "CIDH verifica criminalización y persecución judicial en Nicaragua. Reliefweb (August 2) https://reliefweb.int/report/nicaragua/cidh-verifica-criminalizaci-n-y-persecuci-n-judicial-en-nicaragua.

[129] Perez, O.J. (3 July 2018). "Can Nicaragua's Military Prevent a Civil War?" Foreign Policy https://foreignpolicy.com/2018/07/03/can-nicaraguas-military-prevent-a-civil-war/.

[130] Salazar, M. and López, I. (4 June 2018). "Los escuadrones de la muerte de Ortega." Confidencial https://confidencial.com.ni/los-escuadrones-de-la-muerte-de-ortega/.

[131] See Lessing, B. (2016) Counterproductive Punishment: How Prison Gangs Undermine State Authority", Pearson Institute Discussion Paper No 33, September, https://thepearsoninstitute.org/sites/default/files/2017-02/33.%20Lessing_Counterproductive%20punishment.pdf.

[132] See: http://www.prisonstudies.org/country/brazil. Also see Coyle, A. et al (2016). "Current trends and practices in the use of imprisonment." International Review of the Red Cross, vol. 98 (3), 761–781. DOI: https://doi.org/10.1017/S1816383117000662.

[133] See http://www.prisonstudies.org/highest-to-lowest/occupancy-level?field_region_taxonomy_tid=24.

[134] United Nations Human Rights Council (July 2018). Report of the Special Rapporteur on extrajudicial, summary or arbitrary executions on her mission to El Salvador. Thirty-eighth session https://www.ohchr.org/en/issues/executions/pages/srexecutionsindex.aspx.

[135] A study by Bergman et al (2014) found that more than half of all inmates reported in selected Mexican prisons were in on minor offences (theft of US$280 or less).

[136] The two-way causality between poverty and incarceration rates implies a type of positive feedback loop, where rising incarceration rates create conditions that beget even higher rates of imprisonment (Haney, 2006).Also see See DeFina and Hannon (2013).

[137] See DeFina R. and Hannon L. (2013) "The Impact of Mass Incarceration on Poverty", Crime & Delinquency, Vol. 59.

[138] See the World Female Imprisonment List at prisonstudies.org.

[139] See Safranoff, A. and Tiraasi, A. (2018) Incarcerated Women in Latin America: Characteristics and Risk Factors Associated with Criminal Behavior (Washington DC: BID).

[140] See Dammert, L. (2007) "Seguridad pública en América Latina: ¿qué pueden hacer los gobiernos locales?" Nueva Sociedad 212, pp. 67–81.

[141] See Frühling, H. (2012) La eficácia de las politicas públicas de seguridad ciudadana en América Latina y el Caribe: Como medirla y como mejorarla (Washington, D.C.: BID), https://publications.iadb.org/handle/11319/5688.

[142] See Muggah, R. (2019) "Brazil´s Murder Rate Finally Fell – and by a Lot", Foreign Policy, April 22, https://foreignpolicy.com/2019/04/22/brazils-murder-rate-finally-fell-and-by-a-lot/.

[143] See Forum Brasileiro de Seguraca Publica (http://www.forumseguranca.org.br/wp-content/uploads/2018/08/FBSP_Anuario_Brasileiro_Seguranca_Publica_Infogrpercent C3percentA1fico_2018.pdf).

[144] United Nations Human Rights Council (July 2018). Report of the Special Rapporteur on extra-judicial, summary or arbitrary executions on her mission to El Salvador. Thirty-eighth session https://www.ohchr.org/en/issues/executions/pages/srexecutionsindex.aspx.

[145] Intelligence led policing refers to the use of data and crime intelligence to inform decision making that maximizes police efficiency and effectiveness.

[146] See Alvarado, N., Muggah, R. and Aguirre, K. (2015). "Some Key Good and Bad Takeaways from a Citizen Security Mapping Tool for Latin America", Sin Miedos, 15 October, http://blogs.iadb.org/sinmiedos/2015/10/15/some-key-good-and-bad-takeaways-from-a-citizen-security-mapping-tool-for-latin-america/.

[147] See UNDP (2013) op cit. See also https://igarape.org.br/en/citizen-security-dashboard/.

[148] See, for example, ICG (2013). "Justice at the Barrel of a Gun: Vigilante Militias in Mexico", Latin America Briefing 29, 28 May (Mexico City, Bogotá, Brussels: ICG), https://www.crisis-group.org/latin-america-caribbean/mexico/justice-barrel-gun-vigilante-militias-mexico.

[149] For a comprehensive discussion of the application of contemporary policing strategies in Latin America please see Ungar and Arias (2012).

[150] Major restructuring processes swept across Central and South America over the past two decades, including in Argentina, Colombia's National Police, Chile's Investigative Police and Venezuela, where successive efforts have been undertaken. See FLACSO (2007). "Report on the Security Sector in Latin America and the Caribbean", Santiago de Chile: Facultad Latinoamericana de Ciencias Sociales.

[151] See Muggah, R. and I. Szabo de Carvalho (2014). "Changes in the Neighborhood: Reviewing Citizen Security Cooperation in Latin America", Strategic Paper 7, March https://igarape.org.br/wp-content/uploads/2014/03/AE-07-Changes-in-the-Neighborhood_10th_march.pdf .

[152] Berk-Seligson, S., Orces, D., Pizzolitto, G., Seligson, M., and C. Wilson. (2014). "Impact Evaluation of USAID's Community-Based Crime and Vioelnce Prevention Approach in Central America: Regional Report for El Salvador, Guatemala, Honduras, and Panama." USAID and Vanderbilt University, https://www.vanderbilt.edu/lapop/carsi/Regional_Report_v12d_final_W_120814.pdf.

[153] See Kinosian, S. and Bosworth, J. (2018). "Security for Sale: Challenges and Good Practices in Regulating Military and Security Companies in Latin America", The Dilaogue, March 2018, https://www.thedialogue.org/wp-content/uploads/2018/03/Security-for-Sale-FINAL-ENGLISH.pdf.

[154] See Provost, C. (2017). "The Industry of Inequality: Why the world is obsessed with private security", The Guardian, 12 May https://www.theguardian.com/inequality/2017/may/12/industry-of-inequality-why-world-is-obsessed-with-private-security.

[155] Given the lack of transparency in the industry, it is difficult to precisely determine their numbers: there are roughly 470,000 registered private security personnel in Brazil and at least 450,000 in Mexico. The numbers registered in Bolivia (2002) are 500, 570,000 in Brazil (2005), 45,000 in Chile (2008), 190,000 in Colombia (2005), 19,5000 in Costa Rica (2008), 30,000 in the Dominican Republic (2008), 40,300 in Ecuador (2005), 21,1000 in El Salvador (2008), 120,000 in Guatemala (2008), 60,000 in Honduras (2005), 450,000 in Mexico (2005), 19,7000 in Nicaragua (2008), 30,000 in Panama (2008) and 50,000 in Peru (2005). By way of comparison, the United States is estimated to have at least 2 million as of 2007. See Small Arms Survey (2011: 106); also see Expert Group on Private Security Services, "Civilian Private Security Services: Their Role, Oversight, and Contribution to Crime Prevention and Community Safety", United Nations Office on Drugs and Crime, August 24, 2011, pp. 2–3.

[156] DCAF and the United Nations Regional Centre for Peace, Disarmament and Development in Latin America and the Caribbean (UNLIREC) recently undertook a regional study on armed private security in Latin America and the Caribbean. It found that the private security industry has grown significantly over the last 20 years. The study identified 16,174 private security companies operating in the region, with more than 2,450,000 legal employees working as security guards.

[157] See Muggah and Aguirre (2013) op cit. and Alvarado et al (2015) op cit.

[158] Muggah and Szabo (2014) op cit.

[159] A notable exception is a meta-review conducted by Abt, T. and Winship, C. (2016). "What Works in Reducing Community Violence: A Meta-Review and Field Study for the Northern Triangle." Washington DC: USAID, https://www.usaid.gov/sites/default/files/USAID-2016-What-Works-in-Reducing-Community-Violence-Final-Report.pdf.

[160] See Muggah (2017) op cit. and Aguirre and Muggah (2013) op cit.

161 Ibid.

162 See, for example, the Bogota Manifesto at http://www.iadb.org/en/news/news-releases/2010-04-16/mayors-latin-america-and-the-caribbean-alliance-of-cities-citizen-security-idb,6993.html.

163 For an example of how UPP policies are being adopted in Panama and beyond see Muggah, R. and Mulli, A. (2012). "Rio Tries Counterinsurgency", Current History 111 (742): pp. 62–66.

164 Muggah, Robert (2017) "The Rise of Citizen Security in Latin America and the Caribbean" in Alternative Pathways to Sustainable Development: Lessons from Latin America, International Development Policy series No.9 (Geneva, Boston: Graduate Institute Publications, Brill-Nijhoff). pp. 291–322.

165 See Ortega, D. and Sanguinetti, P. (2014). "Por una América Latina Más Segura." Caracas: CAF. http://scioteca.caf.com/bitstream/handle/123456789/167/reporte-economia-desarrollo-seguridad-control-delito.pdf.

166 Ibid.

167 See Muggah and Szabo (2014) op. cit.

168 See Muggah and Alvarado (2016) op. cit.

169 See, for example, Alvarado, N., Muggah, R. and Aguirre, K. (2015) "Some Good and Bad Takeaways from a Citizen Security Mapping Tool for Latin America", IADB Blog, October 15, https://blogs.iadb.org/seguridad-ciudadana/en/some-key-good-and-bad-takeaways-from-a-citizen-security-mapping-tool-for-latin-america/.

170 See OVE (2014) The Implementation Challenge: Lessons from Five Citizen Security Projects. Washington DC: IADB. https://publications.iadb.org/publications/english/document/The-Implementation-Challenge-Lessons-From-Five-Citizen-Security-Projects.pdf; Berk-Seligson, S., Orc's, D., Pizzolitto, G., Selgson, M., and Ilson, C. (2016) Impact Evaluation of USAID's Community-Based Crime and Violence Prevention Approach in Central America: Regional Report for El Salvador, Guatemala, Honduras and Panaa. Washington DC: USAID and Vanderbilt University, https://www.vanderbilt.edu/lapop/carsi/ExecutiveSummary_CARSI_W_121814.pdf.

171 See Augirre, K. and Muggah, R. (2017) "Multilateral Agencies and Citizen Security Approach in Latin America", Revista CIDOB d'Afers Internacional, 116: pp. 25–52.

172 See Mugah, R. and Aguirre, K. (2013) Mapping Citizen Security Interventions in Latin America: Reviewing the Evidence, NOREF Report, October, https://igarape.org.br/wp-content/uploads/2013/10/265_91204_NOREF_Report_Muggah-Aguirre_web1.pdf.

173 See Muggah et al. (2016).

174 See FIP (2015). "Evaluacion de impacto del Plan Nacional de Vigilancia Comunitaria por Cuadrantes." Bogota: FIP, https://www.oas.org/es/sap/dgpe/innovacion/banco/ANEXO%20II.%20PNVCC.pdf.

175 The idea behind social urbanism was for the municipal government to prioritize building urban infrastructure and providing services in areas of the city that were poorest and most marginalized. See https://www.theglobeandmail.com/news/world/social-urbanism-experiment-breathes-new-life-into-colombias-medellin/article22185134/.

176 See Muggah et. al. (2016) op. cit.

177 See Muggah, R. (2017) "Where Are the World´s Most Fragile Cities", CityLab, November 27, https://www.citylab.com/equity/2017/11/where-are-the-worlds-most-fragile-cities/546782/.

178 Muggah, R. and Szabo, I. (2018), "Violent crime in Sao Paulo has dropped dramatically. Is this why?" Agenda, 7 May, https://www.weforum.org/agenda/2018/03/violent-crime-in-sao-paulo-has-dropped-dramatically-this-may-be-why/.

179 See http://www.rj.gov.br/web/seseg/exibeconteudo?article-id=1444227.

180 See http://www.upprj.com/.

181 See Muggah, R. and Mulli, A. (2012). op cit.

[182] For more on this see Alvarado, N. and Muggah, R. (2016). "Crime and Violence: Obstacles to development in Latin America and Caribbean cities." IDB Cities Network. p. 71. https://igarape.org.br/wp-content/uploads/2018/11/Crimeand-Violence-ObstaclestoDevelopment.pdf.

[183] Ibid. p. 71.

[184] Ibid. p. 71.

[185] Ibid. p. 65.

[186] These include gyms to promote outdoor recreation, swimming pools to promote social mixing, state-of-of-the art boxing facilities to support young people and the creation of a facilitating entity—Convive Feliz—to organize cultural and sporting activities.

[187] Meanwhile, the Linea Verde increased property values by as much as 20 per cent since the intervention was undertaken. There are also signs that the intervention improved overall quality of life through improvements in services and greening the urban environment. There are signs that the Linea Verde initiative may be replicated elsewhere in Mexico and was recently awarded the Guangzhou International Award for Urban Innovation.

[188] For more on this see Alvarado, N. and Muggah, R. (2016). p. 66.

[189] The pilot included 750 police officers trained in improved investigatory and community policing techniques. Funding was also allocated to improving the national police academy´s technological infrastructure, building three police units and disseminating a new police code of ethics.

[190] Alvarado, N. and Muggah, R. (2016). Op cit. p. 66.

[191] Alongside the POP initiative, the Integrated Program for Citizen Security is supporting PADO by helping to further strengthen crime analysis and investigation techniques through training and advanced software.

[192] See Alvarado, N. and Muggah, R. (2016). Op cit. p. 67.

[193] See IADB (2018). "Como evitar el delito urbano? El program de alta deicacion operativa em la nueva policia Urugyaya." Montevideo: IADB. https://publications.iadb.org/bitstream/handle/11319/8858/Como-evitar-el-delito-urbano-el-programa-de-alta-dedicacion-operativa-en-la-nueva-policia-uruguaya.pdf?sequence=1&isAllowed=y.

[194] See Muggah et al (2013), Economist (2017b) and Justus et al (2018).

[195] The chief criticism is that they can afford such groups opportunities to re-arm. In other cases, pacts can allow gangs to shore up their legitimacy and capacity in their communities, especially in the absence of concessions and external verification measures.

[196] See Alvarado, N. and Muggah, R. (2016). Op cit p. 75.

[197] See, for example, Alvarado, N. and Muggah, R. (2018) Un Obstáculo Para el Desarrollo de las Ciudades de América Latina y el Caribe, IADB DP 66, November, https://publications.iadb.org/publications/spanish/document/Crimen-y-violencia-Un-obstaculo-para-el-desarrollo-de-las-ciudades-de-America- Latina-y-el-Caribe.pdf.

www.ingramcontent.com/pod-product-compliance
Lightning Source LLC
Chambersburg PA
CBHW081651270326
41933CB00018B/3430